KILLER

My Life in Hockey

DOUG
GILMOUR
with Dan Robson

HARPERCOLLINS PUBLISHERS LTD

Published by HarperCollins Publishers Ltd

First published by HarperCollins Publishers Ltd in a hardcover edition: 2017
First trade paperback edition: 2018
This mass market paperback edition: 2025

HarperCollins Publishers Ltd
Bay Adelaide Centre, East Tower
22 Adelaide Street West, 41st Floor
Toronto, Ontario, Canada
M5H 4E3

www.harpercollins.ca

HarperCollins Publishers
Macken House, 39/40 Mayor Street Upper
Dublin 1, D01 C9W8, Ireland
https://www.harpercollins.com

Library and Archives Canada Cataloguing in Publication
information is available upon request.

ISBN 978-1-4434-7759-8

Printed and bound in the United States of America
BVG 9 8 7 6 5 4 3 2 1

KILLER

For Dolly and Don Gilmour—Mom and Dad—

for everything you gave me

Contents

KILLER

1

LITTLE GILLY

A person shows what he is by what he does with what he has.

—Anonymous

Long before they ever called me "Killer," I was known as "Little Gilly."

I was only four, maybe five, then. My father was the coach of a bantam all-star team in Kingston, Ontario, where I grew up. His name was Don, but many people around town called him Gilly. Whenever the team played, I went with him, and so they called me Little Gilly. Each time, I'd bring along my skates, and during intermissions Dad would lift me up over the boards and set me down on the ice. I'd wheel around before the ice was cleared. The fans would wait around at the end of each period just to watch me skate—I was like the team's mascot. I had a special team sweater and I wore these massive hockey mitts that didn't fit—they almost took up my entire arms. I didn't know that people were watching me back then. I didn't hear their cheers. I was too busy racing around the big, cold surface—striding and striding . . . and wobbling . . . and striding—around and around, trying to balance the puck on my stick. I would have kept going forever if they'd let me.

One time, during a tournament at Easter, the organizers gave me a trophy for my efforts. It was the first one I'd ever received, and I was thrilled. In fact, I loved it so much that when I went to the same tournament the next year and they gave me a chocolate bunny, I was furious. For most kids, that would have been great. But I didn't want the damn bunny! I wanted a trophy. I wanted to be part of a team—and I wanted to win. I was so sour about it I started to cry.

Let's just say I was a competitive person from the start. That would get me into trouble on more than a few occasions. One time in particular still scares me to this day.

We didn't know how thin the ice was. "First one there wins!" my sister said—and she took off towards the big ship resting on frozen Lake Ontario, about 50 yards from the shoreline. We were supposed to stay close to the rink at the Royal Military College in Kingston. But we were curious kids. I couldn't have been more than 10 years old at the time. We had walked down to the bank beneath old Fort Henry after a game during a weekend hockey tournament, while our parents were still in the arena. They'd told us to stay away from the lake. But the ship was huge and we wanted to see it up close. My sister Donna was a pure tomboy. A year older than me, and taller, too. It wasn't that she was tall for her age. I was just short—and skinny—for mine.

Donna had a head start on me and my pal Ian MacInnis, or we would have had at least a chance of beating her. It wasn't a fair race. And so, Donna was several strides ahead of us when she disappeared.

She went through and didn't come up. Ian and I raced towards the black hole she'd fallen into. I got down on my knees, then lay on my stomach and plunged my arm into the piercing cold water. I searched frantically while Ian held on to my legs. It must have been seconds, but it felt like much longer than that. I thought she was gone, trapped underwater somewhere beneath that thin sheet of ice. That's when I felt her hand tug my arm. I didn't know how I was going to do it, but I knew I needed to get her out. I yelled at Ian to pull and he did. And somehow we heaved Donna out of the lake without going in ourselves. We scrambled to thicker ice, closer to the bank. She was drenched and freezing, getting colder and colder fast. And she was hysterical. She was probably in shock. A man saw us on the ice and came out to help. He helped us back to the arena, shivering and terrified.

Inside the RMC rink, adults covered Donna in blankets, trying to warm her up. That's when we saw our parents coming—and knew that although the worst was over, it was still about to get pretty bad. Mom and Dad had warned us. If they knew what we'd done, we'd be in so much trouble, we'd be as good as dead anyways. Both of us. We had to think quickly.

"Tell them I pushed you in a puddle," I told her. It wasn't the sharpest lie I'd ever come up with. But Donna spun the story, and it worked. Even if Mom and Dad took the opportunity to ground me for a month. (We didn't tell my parents what *really* happened that day until years later, after Donna got married.)

You won't find many idyllic Canadian stories about pond hockey in this book, because ever since that day, I refused to play it. You won't get me close to the ice if I'm not convinced there's a slab of concrete beneath it. Since then, I've just never trusted the ice on a frozen pond or lake. I just can't bring myself to play that picture-perfect game of hockey in the great outdoors. Never will.

Something else stuck with me after the day my sister went through the ice. Even at that young age, I'd already heard time and again that I was too short and too small. It was my flaw. It was the reality that would threaten to keep me from living my dreams of becoming a professional hockey player. But that day on the lake, it didn't matter how small I was. Sure, it was a burst of adrenaline. But it was also a burst of will. I needed strength at that very moment, and I found it.

It must have been there all along.

Of course, even though I knew I had the strength to do more than my stature suggested, it wasn't going to be easy to convince the world of that. And by "world," I mean the *hockey* world. This was Kingston, after all. And in Kingston, hockey was all that mattered.

Kingston is known for being the first capital of the British province of Canada, designated as such when the colonies of Upper and Lower Canada were united in 1841. That only lasted a few years, but the city has served the country in many ways since. My hometown is considered to be one of the birthplaces of hockey. While historians argue about exactly when and where the sport began (there were certainly roots on the East Coast, and the first indoor game is said to have been played in Montreal), Kingston is home to the longest ongoing rivalry in hockey. Back in 1886, students from Queen's College (now Queen's University) challenged a group of students from the Royal Military College to a game on Kingston Harbour. The students had been playing shinny on the lake for a while, but this was the first official match. The annual meeting between the Queen's and RMC varsity teams continues to this day, when the two meet to play for the Carr-Harris Cup. Although, these days they play indoors.

Over the decades, many great hockey players came from Kingston. And when I was growing up, they all seemed to play for the Boston Bruins. Hometown guys Wayne Cashman and Rick Smith both played for the Bruins in the late '60s and early '70s, when the franchise was anchored by the great Bobby Orr. Back then, the Bruins always had their training camp in Kingston—and the team's Senior A affiliate, the Aces, played out of the Memorial Centre on York Street. Seeing the team come through town every year built a strong connection between the city and the franchise. There were certainly a lot of Montreal and Toronto fans in Kingston, which sits almost exactly between both cities. But even today you'll find hold-over Bruins fans from the days when Kingston was the team's training camp home. On top of that, in 1974, another well-known local man entered Bruins lore, taking over as the team's coach: Don Cherry.

Throughout my NHL career, Don would always be a big supporter of mine. But long before he supported me, he coached and was a big fan of another Gilmour—my older brother, David. He's 13 years older than me, and by the time I first started shuffling around on skates, he was already a local legend.

While Dave was chasing his hockey dream, I dreamed of being just like him. I remember going to his games and thinking he was the greatest hockey player ever. One of my first memories in the hockey rink is watching Dad coach the Kingston Hawks midget team. Donna and I would often go along to the games with my mom to watch them.

Dave was an all-around athlete. As all-around as they come. Our house was full of trophies that he won. He was a great baseball player. He could have gone pro. He had the opportunity to try out for the Montreal Expos. But when the time came to decide between a future in hockey or baseball, Dave chose hockey. Dave left home when I was very young to go play for the Peterborough Petes when he was 17. Then he did a stint with the Hamilton Red Wings, before joining the London Knights in 1969—where he was teammates with Darryl Sittler. Then he went on to play in the minors, in places like Rochester, Salt Lake City, Baltimore and Charlotte. Sometimes Dave would bring me some of his old equipment and I'd try to use it. He sent me these skates that were way too big for me, but I stuffed the ends and wore them anyway. They were cool. I wasn't going to let my small feet ruin the chance to brag about how great my brother was.

Honestly, I was in awe watching Dave play. He was a faster skater than I'd ever be. And he was skilled. He'd skate in on a breakaway, look one way and then shoot the other. The goalie would be lucky if he scored, because if the puck hit him it would leave a mark. Dave could unleash a vicious shot. He was tough. On and off the ice, Dave had an edge. That would ultimately be his undoing in the game. He always wanted to play the game his way. That meant that he wasn't much for coaches or instruction, particularly when that instruction came with criticism. One of the biggest lessons I'd learn from him is that attitude is everything. It was a lesson he had to learn the hard way.

I guess I can admit now that I was a bit of a brat back then. It wasn't that I was trying to be bad; I just had a really hot temper. My older sister Debbie (she's a year younger than Dave) used to babysit Donna and me all the time. She definitely had to give me a few swats on the butt. Whenever I got mad at her, I'd run to the closet and sit on a stool that we kept in there. I wouldn't talk to anyone. I'd just shut myself away until I calmed down. Other times, if I was angry, I'd just hold my breath. I don't know what I was trying to accomplish, but it seemed to make sense to me at the time. I was so stubborn that I'd hold my breath until I passed out. Seriously. I'd just black out and my parents or my sister would just wait until I regained consciousness. "Do you feel better?" they'd ask. "Do you know what you were crying about?" And usually, by the time I came to, I'd have no clue.

There was one time I remember crying for a good reason, though. To put it nicely, my parents were frugal. They liked to save money where they could. One of the ways they saved money was on babysitters. Instead of going for the best around when Debbie wasn't available, they went for the cheapest rate available. One time, the lady they had watching me when I was two and a half went to give me a bath but forgot that the hot water had been running for a while. She put my foot in the tub. It was scalding. I screamed. It burned me so bad all the skin came off my foot. Debbie was walking home from the bus when she saw the babysitter running down the street with me wailing in her arms. She had stuck a wool sock on my burnt foot. Debbie grabbed me from her and pulled off the sock. I shrieked. Parts of my foot were so badly burned, she could see the bone. They rushed me to Kingston General Hospital.

They had to do skin grafting to treat my foot. I had to go back to the hospital two or three times a week, and each time I did I'd scream bloody murder.

Thankfully, it healed all right. And it was the only time my parents' thrifty nature really hurt me. In fact, for the most part I benefited from their resourcefulness.

My dad, Don, and mom, Dolly, were both raised in Kingston. We're a "corrections family." Dad spent 32 years of his life working in the prison system in Kingston, and Mom spent 28. Dave and Debbie would later work in corrections as well.

Dad worked at the Kingston Penitentiary, which was the oldest prison in Canada at the time of its closure in 2013. (It first opened in 1835 and was once visited by Charles Dickens.) Dad started as a guard but eventually became the stores keeper, with a staff of inmates that worked for him. The stores keeper was in charge of ordering the food and other goods the prison needed to operate. There was a building outside of the penitentiary where the trucks would come and drop their loads off to be processed. The benefit for us was that Dad often brought home some of the extras. We lived close to the penitentiary, on Metcalfe Avenue, near the city's YMCA. Our place was one of the go-to destinations for kids in the neighbourhood, because we always had a big tub of ice cream in the freezer. Like a giant, parlour-sized tub that Dad would bring home from the pen. And we had monkey bars that Dad had the inmates help with. We also had a pool table in the basement that doubled as a Ping-Pong table when Dad would put a wood top on it. Back then, a tub of ice cream, monkey bars and endless Ping-Pong made you one of the most popular kids on the street!

Sometimes the stuff Dad brought home from the prison was a bit odd. Our patio furniture in the backyard was made out of an old steel gurney he took from the prison's medical ward. It sat low to the ground, and Dad put a piece of foam on it in place of the mattress. He also brought home this painting of a topless mermaid that an inmate painted for him. Dad thought it was the greatest thing. He hung it above our fireplace.

Dad was always looking for ways to make an extra buck. He would buy used cars for about $1,000 and park them in our garage. There were always several cars in our driveway or lined up beside the house. He'd fix them up (or not at all, in some cases) and turn around and sell them for $1,200 a week later. Then he'd stash the money in one of several boxes he hid around the house. I don't know why he was obsessed with doing that, but he always did—even later in life. He always needed to have cash hidden away. He kept about $100 in his wallet, but he'd never use it. He just needed to have the money in his wallet. He'd go to the drugstore carrying the money, but he wouldn't use it to buy anything. He was just funny like that.

While Dad loved watching and coaching hockey, he wasn't much of a player himself. When he was growing up in Kingston, baseball was his thing. He was a catcher. And so baseball was a big part of my life growing up. Dad was a Yankees fan for life, but also a Montreal Expos fan because the team was relatively close to Kingston. So I grew up as an Expos fan, too. I remember the first trip he took me on to Jarry Park in Montreal. I was eight years old. It was so exciting to see my favourite players take the field in front of me. Guys like Rusty Staub and Ron Fairly. Seeing them in person was better than I could imagine. I'll never forget when I was waiting to get in line at the stadium, this one guy ahead of me said, "Shit before shovel," and let me go in first. It took me a moment to get it, but it made me laugh.

My father worked incredibly hard. And because he worked hard, he loved his weekends. On Saturday evenings, it was always *Hockey Night in Canada*—that's when he and his buddies would get together. We usually hosted the house parties. Dad's friends would bring their kids and we'd all watch together in the living room while they had a few beers. It could be Montreal, Toronto or Boston playing. It didn't matter to us. It was hockey, so we didn't care who was on the ice. The kids would play hockey in the basement with mini-sticks between periods. The Saturday night games in those days weren't over until close to 11 p.m. Halfway through the third period, we kids were usually all out cold, asleep on the floor.

While I loved baseball, too, hockey quickly became my life. I started playing as soon as I was old enough, and it was pretty much an everyday thing. There were pickup games all over the place, whether you were lacing up the skates or just playing with your boots on. There was a school within 15 yards of our house, and all the neighbourhood kids would meet up there. We'd play for hours. Sometimes we'd turn on the taps outside the school to try to get a drink of water; when they were shut off, somebody would go home and get a jug for everyone. We'd forget about eating. We'd just be out there, running and playing and not caring about anything else in the world. Games involved a lot of offence and very little defence. It wasn't competitive. It was just fun.

When I started playing competitive hockey, one of the things I enjoyed the most was the travel we'd get to do every weekend. There was no team bus, so the parents always drove. Our games were on the weekends—often in Belleville and Trenton, about an hour away, while the others were out an hour and a half to two hours, in cities like Oshawa and Peterborough.

Often, when we played the teams that were farther away from Kingston, we'd arrange a couple of home-and-home series. We'd travel one weekend, stay in town and play a couple games. A couple of weeks later, that team would come to Kingston and we'd host them for two games. One of the teams we did that with was Whitby. To cut down on costs, we arranged with the Whitby team to stay with one of their families during the weekend we played, and then they would stay with us when they came to Kingston. It just so happened that the player I stayed with in Whitby was a goalie named Glenn Healy.

Healy was a great goalie, even then. His family had a little games room in their basement, with a dartboard and stuff like that. They had a gathering of players over after our game. And when I was down in the basement, someone threw a dart that stuck right in my back. It hurt like hell. I didn't find out who it was until I played in the NHL—and faced Healy for the first time. "Remember that dart when you were a kid?" he said. All that time, and I never knew. Healy really played the long game. But that's okay. I'd go on to score on him a few times in my career.

Dad coached me in minor hockey, just like he did with David. He made me a defenceman because they always get more ice time. Back then, we usually had only four defencemen on a team. If one of us got a penalty, a forward would have to drop back to the blue line. That was the old days.

We used to play out of Cooks Arena, north of Kingston's downtown. Back then, rinks didn't even have glass; just chicken wire around the boards. Game days were always a family affair. My dad behind the bench, and my mother and sister Donna in the stands. Even though my mother was a kind and gentle person, especially with her kids, she became something else entirely when one of us was being targeted.

In fact, my mom was something of a local legend at the rink. There are several tales about Dolly Gilmour. One time, when my brother was playing in Kingston's Memorial Centre, she got mad at a referee who called a bad penalty on him. She expressed her anger by grabbing a stick from the team's bench, walking to the edge of the boards and hooking the referee as he skated by. Another time, when David was playing midget, the story goes, he was sent to the box after drilling an opponent into the boards. The team's coach went after my brother and grabbed him by the shoulder. Dolly didn't like that very much. She took off her shoe and threw it at the coach, hitting him right in the head. The next day, when my dad was at work, he received a package full of mismatched women's shoes. An attached note, signed by a co-worker, read, "Now your wife doesn't have to throw her own shoes around."

Mom was actually a great athlete herself. She played basketball at Kingston Collegiate and Vocational Institute, where she went to high school in downtown Kingston, next to the Queen's University campus. She was also a figure skater.

Between my parents, she was the softy. Dad could be hard on us. He was less patient and pretty strict. If we had to confess to something we'd done, we'd go straight to her. "Okay," she'd say. "Don't tell your father." Whatever it was, you never told Dad first, because he'd get friggin' mad. If we needed anything, Mom was the one to go to. If we needed money or wanted something, she said, "Here—but don't tell your father!"

Dad believed in tough love. If we were playing catch, he'd throw a baseball at us. He didn't care if it knocked the wind out of you or hit you right in the face. You had to get right back in there and try it again. It sounds mean, but I think it made us stronger. And I was a stubborn little guy. I could have tears running down my face, but I wasn't going to admit that it hurt. I'd want Dad to throw the ball even harder. I wanted to prove how tough I was.

If we ran into a schoolyard bully, Dad wanted us to fight it out. He didn't want us to come home crying.

"Go stand up for yourself," he'd say.

That might have been the beginning of the determination I'd carry with me through life. Faced with a challenge, I was going to finish it. From that age, all the way through to the end of my hockey career, I'd keep going until I couldn't possibly go anymore.

I don't want you to get the wrong idea. My father was a good man. He was just very demanding. As a dad and as a coach. He wanted his players to know that there was much more to the game than scoring goals. He wanted us to find a way to make our dreams possible. It was about determination.

And I can still remember the taste of determination when I was young. It was supposed to taste like vanilla, but it reminded me more of chalk.

My dad made me drink two cans of Ensure every day. The only thing it guaranteed was that it made me want to throw up. God, I hated that stuff. I was 13 years old, five foot two and 105 pounds. The extra calories I took in each day with that meal-in-a-can stuff was supposed to pack on the weight I needed to prove to scouts that I was big enough to play junior hockey.

At dinner at our home in Kingston, those cans of Ensure were usually accompanied by a plate of mashed potatoes. I hated mashed potatoes, too. But there they were, almost every day—giant scoops of grey, starchy mush. Yuck. Whenever my dad would lift his newspaper up to read at the kitchen table, I'd spoon them beneath my plate or grab a handful of the stuff and stick it in my pocket. I'd squish more in each time he looked away. Mom saw me do it. She knew what I was up to but wasn't about to spoil my plan. After dinner, I'd go to the bathroom and flush the potatoes down the toilet.

All those extra calories didn't do much, unfortunately. Even when I didn't pull off the mashed-mush caper on my dad, I didn't get any bigger. I had skill, but I was puny—and that small fact was going to be a huge obstacle to overcome.

To this day, I still don't eat mashed potatoes. But I think my hockey career turned out all right.

It wasn't easy, though. And as much as I complained about my father's philosophies on adolescent nutrition, I have to give him credit for everything I was fortunate enough to accomplish on the ice. Don Gilmour believed his son could play in the big leagues. And he knew the kind of player I needed to be to get there.

Even when it seemed like the team had done well, he'd give it to us if he thought we hadn't played hard enough. I remember one time, after I'd scored four points in a game, we pulled into our driveway and I was waiting for him to open up the trunk with the key so I could get my equipment. But instead, he just walked towards the house.

"Leave it in there," he said. "You didn't do anything tonight."

I was confused.

"I scored two goals and got two assists!" I objected.

"But you didn't try," he replied and walked into the house.

So I followed him inside and left my gear out in the cold car. What had I done wrong? I couldn't figure it out. The very next game, I didn't score any points. When we got home, I just walked towards the house, assuming my dad would be even more frustrated with my play. But he got out of the car and called to me.

"Whoa, whoa, son," he said. "Come here. Grab your stuff."

I didn't know what to say.

"That's the best that I've ever seen you play," he said. "You worked hard and you had good chances. You didn't get any points—but you *worked.* That's the best I've seen you work."

I realized that he hadn't made me leave my gear in the car to be mean. He was trying to teach me a lesson. He was trying to help me understand the game better. That was just his way of doing it. I learned then that hockey really wasn't just about getting points. It was about work ethic. It was about effort. And about being part of a team. I carried that lesson with me through the rest of my hockey career, and afterwards, in my life. It was one of the most important lessons I learned, one that would help define me as a player and would always be something I'd strive for as a person.

2

SEVENTH-ROUND PICK

The first trip I ever took to Maple Leaf Gardens was when I was 13, to watch my brother play. Dave had signed with the Calgary Cowboys of the World Hockey Association, and his first exhibition game was against the Toronto Toros. I drove with my parents and my friend Rob to Toronto. I was so excited to be there. Just walking into the famous hockey rink gave me goosebumps. The arena felt *enormous*. I was so proud that my big brother was going to be playing there. But when the players came out onto the ice for warm-ups, I couldn't see Dave anywhere. We didn't know where he was. The game started, and he still wasn't on the bench. We sat in the last row of our section, and partway through the first he came up and stood behind us. Dave had been cut from the team, and he was pissed. He said he'd had enough of being shipped around the minors.

"I'm done," he said.

My dad wasn't happy about that. He wanted Dave to keep going. But I knew my brother meant it. He was done with the game. After spending five years chasing his dream through the ranks of minor pro hockey, he just didn't have it in him anymore.

We left the game before the end of the first. Dave gave Rob and me some Cowboys sticks so we could cut them down and use them. We left the Gardens and Dave climbed into our Jeep Wagoneer with us, and we all drove home to Kingston together.

After that, Dave was there to watch me play. He helped me out as much as he could.

When I was getting closer to junior hockey, Dave would give me advice whenever he saw me drifting down the same path he had.

"Don't do what I did," he'd tell me, whenever I was mad at a coach or felt I'd been slighted in some way. "Suck it up. It goes by too quick."

Sometimes his work ethic wasn't there when he was younger, so he was always on me to push myself. And although he had lots of skill, coaches along the way tried to get even more out of him. Dave didn't like that. He wanted to do his own thing; he wanted to do it his own way. Now he was telling me to absorb everything I was told along the way.

I had a chip on my shoulder. In hockey, I was always the best player on the ice, but there were constant whispers that I was too small and would never make it in junior, let alone to the NHL. When I was 15 I went to a pre-season tryout camp with the Belleville Bulls, then a Tier II Junior A team, about an hour west of Kingston. But I didn't make the team. I went back home to play for the Kingston Voyageurs, the local Junior B team. I was only there for about a month. The coach didn't think I was good enough to play ahead of the other players, so I spent most of my time sitting on the bench. I guess I was too small for the coach, especially as a defenceman. I wanted to prove him wrong, but there was nothing I could do if I wasn't being given a shot. And I wasn't learning anything sitting on the bench. After about a month, I asked for my release and decided to go back and play for the Kingston Canadians major midget team. I didn't know what would happen next.

Around the same time, my parents had moved from our four-level side-split in the city to a two-bedroom cottage on Loughborough Lake, about 20 minutes from Kingston. Dad had always wanted a place on the water to retire to. He was happy at the cottage. He'd just find something to do in the garage and be happy there. Or he'd work on fixing up his dock, tying on all these tires he'd collected with random pieces of rope. Or he'd putter around in his boat, fishing for hours, impatiently moving from spot to spot. He lived for the lake; it was his idea of paradise.

I slept on the couch and my sister Donna got the other room. We had a lot of fun there. Dan Aykroyd had a family place just a few doors down from us. The Blues Brothers were huge at the time. They'd have parties with all kinds of celebrities, like John Candy, and Donna and I would often peer through his fence, trying to get a look. We never saw anything. One time, I was on the dock and Dan and John Belushi pulled up in one of those boats that are also cars that can drive on land, too. Little did I know then that Dan and I would become good buddies later on.

I ended up skating with the Kingston Canadians for only two practices. A local scout named Larry Mavety had stepped in to take over the Belleville Bulls, who had gotten off to a dismal start to their season. Larry was looking to change things up with the team, so he called up my dad and asked if I could join them.

When my brother retired from hockey, he began working in the prison system, just like my dad and mom and my older sister Debbie. David was the sports coordinator at Millhaven maximum-security prison, about a 30-minute drive west from Kingston. The inmates had their own baseball teams that would play against each other, but every few weeks he'd bring in a team of local players from our men's league to give the inmates some new competition. After my first year of junior, when I was 17, my brother arranged to have a group of us come in and play a couple of games against their team. I'd played fast-pitch softball my entire life and was pretty good. I figured I could hold my own with a bunch of inmates.

At Millhaven, you enter through these massive steel gates, and then you're in secure—as in, you're not getting out unless they know about it. From the field, we could see a couple of guards in the surveillance towers on the walls. Inmates who weren't playing sat in the bleachers, booing and heckling us. There were some good ballplayers in the group. We were playing underhand fast-pitch, and their pitcher could pitch the ball from behind his back.

When I went up to bat, he threw three pitches above my head. The umpire called each one of them a strike! He was this enormous guy, about six foot seven. I swore at him as I left the plate. My brother pulled me aside when I got to our bench.

"What did you say to him?" he asked.

"I said those were bullshit calls."

"Yeah, well," he said, "that guy's in here because he killed his wife, chopped her up and put her in the freezer."

I didn't say another word for the rest of the game.

After that first season in Belleville, I was drafted in the third round of the Quebec Major Junior Hockey League draft by the Cornwall Royals, by a man named Gord Wood.

Gord was the guy who made me switch from being a defenceman to a forward. I had played on the blue line my whole life, until I got to Cornwall. I was about five foot nine back then, and when I jumped on the scale I came in at around 145 pounds. Gord said, "We've got to move this guy up." It was his decision, really. When he scouted me as a defenceman he knew he wanted me up front because of my playmaking ability.

I was excited to go to Cornwall. They had won the Memorial Cup the year before and still had a great team. Dale Hawerchuk was back after lighting up the league the season before, scoring 37 goals and 107 points. Sixteen-year-old rookie Scott Arniel was also on the team. And our captain was Marc Crawford.

Back then, the Memorial Cup winner represented Canada at the World Junior Championship, so at Christmastime we got to go to Germany as a team. I remember that at the time, my eyebrows were just growing back after they'd been shaved off in our rookie initiation. A bald spot had also been shaved in the middle of my head, with the hair on the sides making me look like I had male pattern baldness. So now I associate looking ridiculous with my first-ever trip abroad.

The tournament was in a place called Landsberg, about an hour outside of Munich, a cute little town with all stone roads. We would practise every day, and then we'd play a game every other day. On the days we didn't play, we'd go off and do something educational. If we had two days off, we'd go on longer educational trips. It was so eye-opening. I took a bunch of Polaroid photos because I had never seen anything like it before. I thought I had to capture everything because I'd probably never see anything like it again. We got to take a tour through the Alps, where we saw all these incredible castles, like you'd see in a Disney film. We also went to a Christmas market in Munich, and I bought this ugly blanket with a Denver Broncos logo on it—I have no idea why. And I bought my mom some wooden plates that had pictures of a castle on them. I had very bad taste.

The most memorable experience was visiting the concentration camps in Dachau. We had to walk a long way just to get there—at the time, people in Germany didn't want anything to do with it, so the bus driver would only drive us to a certain point. We walked through a fence and over a massive ditch, and through another fence. It was all covered in barbed wire. Inside, we toured the bunks where people had been held and the gas chambers where they were killed. That was an education that made everything else in life seem pretty damn small. It's something I've never forgotten.

Before the World Juniors, we'd picked up five other players from the Quebec league—a goalie, a defenceman and three forwards—so I ended up being dropped back to the fourth line. We got to wear Team Canada sweaters, which was very cool (back then they were blue and white, almost like the Toronto Maple Leafs' sweaters). In Germany, our coach ran with three lines most of the time. The rink was half outdoor and half indoor, so it was freezing. One end of the rink was open and the sun lit it up, so it was also bright. During the games, we fourth-liners all sat on the bench, covered in blankets, shivering our butts off. I didn't play much at all. Still, it was a great, albeit cold, experience.

In the end, we didn't do very well. These teams were the elite of the elite from their countries. We were just the junior team that had won the season before. And six of our players from that championship team had left. Russia beat us. The U.S. beat us—they had Craig Ludwig and Bobby Carpenter on the team but finished only one point ahead of us in the standings. West Germany beat us too. We tied Czechoslovakia. The only team we beat was Austria.

Still, we made the most of our European adventure. We stayed three to a room in the dorms there, each sleeping in our own small cot. And we had a tight curfew. It felt like we were under lock and key. But we managed to get out to some bars while our chaperones let their guard down. The German girls we met were beautiful. And because I was still only 17, getting to order a big stein of beer was pretty damn cool.

That first year in Cornwall, I lived in a billet home with another kid from Kingston. He was a goalie named Brian Abrams. He was a Christian guy, and I remember picking up one of the books he had in his room. It was full of quotes. I remember flipping through it, and one stuck with me: "A person shows what he is by what he does with what he has." I never forgot it. I've lived by that my whole life. Every time someone would say, "He's too small; he's not going to make it," that's what fed me the whole time.

Since I was a kid, I've been told I wasn't big enough. In junior, I realized how little I was compared to the other guys, but I wouldn't let it bother me. I would go out and do what I had to do to compete and to survive. And I had to be smart. I wasn't going to put myself into bad situations where the guys were, strength-wise, going to move me around. I had to be the smartest player on the ice if I was going to make it. And I was going to have to play hard. I wasn't called Killer yet, but even back then, once I put my helmet on, my eyes would change, my focus would change—it was an all-out war.

The Royals moved from the Quebec junior league to the Ontario Hockey League before my second season with the team. The move didn't go over well with the fans. Most of the city of Cornwall was French. Our attendance had been about 3,000 fans per game. After the move to the Ontario loop, it dropped by probably 1,000. Part of the problem with the move was that the Royals had to draft out of Ontario, not Quebec, which meant that there would be fewer French players to cheer for. For whatever the reason, it was never really the same in Cornwall after the team made the switch.

That season, Hawerchuk left the team to play for the Winnipeg Jets, after going first overall in the NHL draft. The Jets also took Scott Arniel in the second round. Arniel played half the year in Winnipeg and half the year down with us in Cornwall. That opened a spot for me at centre on the second line, with a chance to occasionally play on the top line. I know it sounds cliché, but timing is everything. If it weren't for the right timing, I don't believe I would have had the career that I did.

Everything really opened up for me in the 1981–82 season. In 67 games, I had 46 goals and 73 assists for 119 points. That season was a lot of fun off the ice as well. I was 18 years old, which was great when you lived on the border of New York State, where that was the legal drinking age at the time. The Royals paid us a weekly stipend. My first season, it was about $20 a week. It was like being given an allowance. On that much, in those days, you could maybe go out for a night, but then the money was gone. The bar scene in New York State was only about 25 minutes away, just over the border bridge. Several of the players on the team had their own cars, so we made the trip regularly. The dad from my first billet family worked for border security, so getting back into Canada was easy. We'd pull up and he'd see us and just wave us through. We wouldn't drink and drive, but we did pack the car pretty tight. There would be about six of us at a time, but there were always at least two of us who weren't drinking. We went to this place called Charlie's in the town of Massena every Tuesday, because they had a 10-cent draught special, which they'd serve in these small plastic cups. We each had about $20 in our pocket, so we could stretch that a long way in a night.

It was just a different time, different days. Some of the best times we had playing for the Royals were those long trips we spent on the road, travelling across Ontario. We'd play in cities like London, Sudbury, Sault Ste. Marie, Windsor, all over the place. Often, one of the players would have parents who lived in the town we visited. After games, we carried our own bags to the bus. Anyone who had family at the game would stop by their parents' car on the way, grab a case of beer out of the trunk and pack it in their bag before loading it back onto the bus. We always stayed in these roadside motels, the ones that had beds that would vibrate for a quarter. We'd have at least three players to a room, with one or two of us sleeping on a cot. Back then, we had to keep our gear with us in the room, so it basically smelled like a locker room in there. Whenever we found out which room had the beer, we'd sneak into the hall and everyone would congregate in front of the door to that room. We managed to have quite a few late-night gatherings that way. Those were the good times.

I remember one time when we were in Sudbury overnight at the same time as the Ottawa 67's. We had played that night and were on our way to the Soo in the morning, and they were playing the Wolves the next day. They were staying at the same hotel as us, so I met up with a couple of their players, John Odam and Doug Stewart. We didn't usually fraternize with other teams, but I had played with John back in Kingston, so we were buddies. So I was in their room, having some beers late into the night, and we were telling stories about our teams, when there was a knock on the door. I panicked and ran into the shower and hid behind the curtain while they answered the knock. It was Brian Kilrea, the legendary coach of the 67's, checking in to make sure his players weren't up past curfew.

You may know that Kilrea was given the nickname "Killer" long before I had it, so this was not a guy I wanted to get busted by. He came in and searched around and said, "Okay, you guys are fine," and left. I dodged that one. So, of course, we had a few more beers to celebrate. About an hour later, they said, "We're going down to the assistant coach's room." That seemed like a strange idea, if not outright dangerous. But they assured me that Kilrea had gone to bed; we were in the clear. So we went down to the room, where an assistant coach and a couple guys from the team's management and scouting staff were hanging out. I was scared. I told the guys I shouldn't be there, but they insisted I stick around. And they had a bucket of KFC and more beer, so I decided, hey, why not. Everyone else, including the coach and management, was long asleep, I figured. Around 2 a.m., I went to leave, and as I opened the door, my coach, Bob Kilger, was standing there, ready to knock. My heart stopped. "It's a little late," he said. "Who's in there?" I told him it was the other team's coach, and then he said okay and just let me go. I turned back and saw he was going into the room to join them.

After a successful season, I was hoping I'd be drafted into the NHL that year. I didn't expect to be a top pick, but I thought

I had a very good chance of being selected. There were several good players in the draft. Brian Bellows went second overall to the Minnesota North Stars, after the Boston Bruins took Gord Kluzak with the first pick. Scott Stevens went fifth to the Washington Capitals, just ahead of Phil Housley, who went to the Buffalo Sabres. Buffalo also selected my future linemate, Dave Andreychuk, who played for the Oshawa Generals, with the 16th pick.

I had led the Royals in scoring, but a couple of my teammates were selected well ahead of me. Our best defenceman, Jim Kyte, went 12th overall to the Winnipeg Jets. One of my good friends, Brent Loney, went 62nd to Edmonton. I was happy for both of them; they both deserved it. They were both incredibly tough. Loney was probably six foot two, 195 pounds. Tough as nails. And boy, could he fight. They both could. But it was frustrating for me because they were a lot bigger than I was, and in those days that was the kind of player NHL teams would pick. Eventually, the St. Louis Blues selected me in the seventh round, 134th overall. Today, I get that I was lucky; most guys never get to experience the honour of being drafted by an NHL team. But back then, I took my seventh-round selection as an insult. I didn't understand why my teammates had been drafted higher than me. It wasn't right, and I held a grudge. I felt that my own team hadn't done enough to promote me to NHL scouts. Back then, everything was driven by word of mouth. Coaches would tell scouts what they thought of their players. That, and maybe a couple of games they attended, was the only way scouts could get a sense of your ability.

I had a huge chip on my shoulder when I went to the Royals' training camp that September. I just wasn't happy. The draft had bruised my ego and I didn't take it well. As part of camp every season, we'd have an intrasquad game that was attended by about 2,000 fans who were given free admission as a promotion to generate interest in the team. During the game, I got into a fight with one of the rookies trying to make the team. I grabbed him by the face mask and ripped his helmet off his head. Then I started hitting him with it. Our own fans booed me as the ref escorted me off the ice. It was ugly. My brother was at the game, and he pulled me aside with some stern advice afterwards.

"Settle down," he said. "Just listen—and get better."

A couple days later, I left Cornwall to attend my first pro camp with the St. Louis Blues in Regina, Saskatchewan.

I knew at the time there was no chance that I was going to make the team that season. Players rarely went straight to the NHL after being drafted from junior back then. But that week was still an incredible experience for me. I was skating with veteran pros for the first time. I had the chance to feel what it was like to play the game at the highest level. The whole time, I knew that this was where I belonged. It made me resent that I was going to have to return to play another season in Cornwall. After practice, I'd hang out with guys like Brian Sutter, Bernie Federko and Mike Liut, just drinking beer with them in the hotel, soaking in the wisdom. There was no curfew for the guys who were already on the team, but kids like me had to be in by 11 p.m. On my last night there, I was out with a bunch of the players, but then all the young guys had to head back to the hotel. One of the scouts made sure we got into our rooms and didn't break curfew. But I decided, "Ah, what the hell." I was going to go back out with the guys. As soon as I closed the door, I climbed out the window, hung on to the edge and dropped down onto a roof one floor down, above the pool. But I hadn't really planned my escape. The roof over the pool was about 25 feet above the ground—and there was no way down, aside from jumping. I was stuck. My only way back into the hotel was to knock on the window to one of the rooms on the floor below mine. A startled couple opened up for me.

"Um, St. Louis Blues . . . initiation," I explained. "Can you let me through?"

My plans were spoiled. I wasn't going to get out of the hotel through the lobby, so I decided to head back to my room. When I walked into the hallway on my floor, the scout who had just walked me to my room a couple of minutes before was still standing there. He looked incredibly confused.

"Hey, sir," I said, as I walked past him. "Have you been drinking?"

The experience of my first NHL training camp only made me more bitter when I returned to Cornwall. The fans were still mad at me for how I'd behaved in the intrasquad game before I'd left. It was a terrible way to start my final season in junior. And it was about to get worse.

Through the first three games of the season, I only had a point or two and wasn't playing very well. I was frustrated. During a game against the Kitchener Rangers at home in Cornwall, I took that frustration out on one of their players. That wasn't smart. I picked a fight with a guy named Mike Eagles. He broke my nose and cracked an orbital bone. I finished the game, but it was bad. I was going to have to go to Kingston to get surgery to repair my face. My parents and brother were in the stands for the game. We all drove back to Kingston together. David snickered the entire time. My nose was basically sideways. He thought it was hilarious. My parents told me I needed to smarten up. I wasn't playing my game, and I was getting into stupid fights. I couldn't object. When your face is half caved in, your nose looks like it was drawn by Picasso and your eyes are black and bloodshot, there isn't much you can say.

Three days after surgery to fix my nose, I was back on the ice, wearing a full face mask. It was an important lesson learned the hard way.

That season, I moved in with my teammate Brent Loney, a hometown player who had gone 62nd overall in the draft. Brent was a very good hockey player, but he was also a great guy. He had a little four-door Chevy that we used to drive around in. We installed an eight-track player and used to drive around town, listening to Boxcar Willie songs. His parents did shift work, so sometimes they weren't home after our games, so we got the house to ourselves.

The rink's Zamboni driver lived a few doors down from the Loney house. He was about 10 years older than us, and we used to get him to buy us beer and he'd hang out with us. We'd have three or four guys over, just having some pizza and a couple of beers. It was nothing crazy, but always a good time. One night, after one of our games, Brent and I were hanging out in the basement with a couple of our teammates. His parents were both at work, on their shifts. The Zamboni driver came by and asked if we wanted to go and grab some food with him at a nearby truck stop called the Fifth Wheel. We'd already had some pizza, and I wasn't very hungry, so I decided not to go.

The truck stop was only about 10 minutes away. I remember thinking it was taking them a while—and then the phone rang. It was the police. There'd been an accident. The car had jumped railroad tracks, hit some ice and slammed into the mast supporting the gate. The passenger's side was totalled. Loney wasn't moving when the first responders got to the scene. He was alive, they said, but unconscious. He was in a coma.

I didn't know how to react. I had to contact his parents at work and tell them what had happened. They were angry; they were in shock. They wanted to know why I wasn't with him. No one else in the car had been injured. They were in a state of panic, not sure if their son would live or die. I didn't know what to say.

We went to the hospital, where Loney was in his hospital bed, attached to machines, not moving. I'll never forget it. It was devastating. His parents were a mess. Our team was a mess. Our coach wanted to know what had happened. Everyone was looking for a reason, but there wasn't one. It was just an accident; nobody did anything wrong. It was scary for all of us. I was 19 years old and an elder statesman on the team, and it was very possible that my good friend and roommate was never coming back. At that age, it's difficult to process things like that happening.

We were left in that uncertainty for several days. Then Brent woke up. It seemed like a miracle. He was hurt very badly and was going to take a long time to recover—but he was going to recover. Brent even returned to play 47 games with us and went on to play a few games in the International and American leagues.

Looking back at it now, I never really had a regular high school experience. Because I lived with billets, I was all over the place. In my first year, I went to St. Lawrence High School, and then the second year, I went to Cornwall Collegiate. In my second year, I had one of those teachers you never forget. He was this tall guy with really long hair, about 40 years old. He was incredibly eccentric, so naturally, he was a philosophy teacher. For his class, I had to write an essay—I think it was on John Locke, or someone like that. Well, after I handed it in, I ran into him at this chicken wing place in town called Coco's. I was there with some guys from the team, having some wings and some beer—so I went over and bought him a pint. Different times, back then. It turned out to be the best move of my academic career. When I got back my paper a few days later, I got 100 per cent. Who gets 100 per cent on a philosophy paper? Not me, that's for sure! I loved that guy—he was just a different dude.

After moving in with the Loneys in my last year, I went to another school called General Vanier. I'll lay one thing out here: school was not really my thing. It's not that I didn't get it or that I didn't want to work hard. I spent summers doing extra courses at LCVI in Kingston, just to make sure I was on track to graduate after a busy hockey season. If anything, junior hockey players have to work extra hard, be disciplined and manage their time effectively if they want to do well in school and on the ice. That's why student-athletes often go on to do well in their professions after their playing days are done. But that last year, I had just had enough. I was only looking to complete my Grade 13 courses (some of you reading this might remember when Ontario had Grade 13). School wasn't really on my mind anymore. We had to be at the rink every morning, and then there would be class from 8:30 to noon every day. It was too much. I had a locker at General Vanier for about a week, and then I was like, "I'm not going to do this. I'm going to focus on hockey."

My only goal that year was to prove the world wrong about my potential to play the game.

In 1980–81, the Royals had gone to the World Juniors to represent Canada. It was the last time that format was used. The following season, an all-star team from across the country was selected, which is the system in place to this day. After my great start to my final season in junior, I was invited to the selection camp for the Canadian junior national team in Toronto. Excited for the opportunity, I took a flight down from Ottawa, hoping I'd get the chance to represent my country. I hadn't been invited to the camp that summer, but I still thought I had a good chance of making the team. At that point, I had scored points in just over 20 consecutive games.

The Leafs played at 8 p.m. on Saturday night, and when the game was over we had a scrimmage at the Gardens. We didn't get on the ice until around 11 p.m. We got back to the hotel a couple of hours later, and then had to be back at the Gardens for 8 a.m. and on the ice by nine. We were playing on almost no sleep. It was exhausting. Around 11 a.m., the coaches called me into their room. There were a few of us lined up outside the room. They called me in and it was "Thank you for coming, but you didn't make it." It had been only 12 hours since I first stepped on the ice! It all happened that quickly.

I was pissed. It seemed pretty clear to me they had already made up their minds about who was going to be on the team, and they just wanted to make it look like they were taking a look at a few of us who were having a good start to the year. I remember that, as I was walking out, I asked one of the team managers if I could have my passport back. My parents had mailed it in to Hockey Canada when I was invited, so that they could arrange travel. I assumed it had been brought to Toronto because the team was leaving for Russia the next day. "I don't think we have it," the guy said. "It's not here." I was sure right then that there was never going to be a spot for me on the team anyway. It was all just a show. Just another kick in the nuts.

I had somebody drive me to the airport in Toronto for my flight back to Ottawa, where I was picked up and driven to Cornwall for the start of our Sunday night game, just in time to keep my scoring streak alive. My parents were at the game and drove me home afterwards so I could spend the holiday break in Kingston. I remember that they were just livid. "If they had the teams picked, why would you even go and waste your time?" my dad asked. They were incredulous.

But in the end, I think, being excluded from the World Junior team wasn't a bad thing. The Christmas break was a great time to collect my thoughts and get ready to have a great second half of the season. At that time, I just wanted to keep playing well, have a great playoff run—and set myself up for my first contract with the St. Louis Blues.

Things worked out pretty well. I continued my scoring streak, recording at least one point in 57 consecutive games, breaking the OHL record of 52, set by Jim Fox of Ottawa in 1979–80. I finished with 70 goals and 107 assists for 177 points. The second-highest scorer in the league had 148 points. I won the Eddie Powers Trophy as the OHL's leading scorer and was awarded the Red Tilson Trophy as the league's most outstanding player.

We lost to the Ottawa 67's—led by goalie Darren Pang, who stood on his head—in the league quarter-finals, and just like that, my junior hockey career was over. But I felt pretty good. My plan was to play with the Blues the following season. I'd proven my critics wrong; I'd proven that I belonged. I was going to the NHL. My dream was about to come true. But three months later, I found myself playing for a team in Düsseldorf, Germany—not sure where exactly my hockey career would take me next.

3

"DREI PILSNER, BITTE!"

After my junior career ended, I was excited to get my shot to play in the NHL. The St. Louis Blues weren't really a great team, which in the end was good news for me. They had won only 25 games in 1982–83 and finished fourth in the Norris Division before being knocked out of the playoffs by the Chicago Blackhawks in the first round. Looking at the roster, I felt like I had a pretty decent shot at making an impact right away. Still, the team had potential, led by some very good players, including Brian Sutter, Bernie Federko and Jorgen Pettersson, "the Handsome Swede."

The downside was that the Blues franchise was a mess. Despite having a stable average attendance of about 13,000, the team couldn't make money. The Blues' owners, Ralston Purina—the Missouri-based animal feed and pet food company—decided they wanted out of the hockey business. The Blues had been in St. Louis since the first NHL expansion in 1967, and the NHL wanted to keep the team in town. However, finding a new owner who wanted the team to stay in St. Louis proved difficult.

There was a serious effort to move the Blues to Saskatoon, led by William "Wild Bill" Hunter, who had been the owner, general manager and eventually coach of the WHA's Alberta Oilers—the team that became the Edmonton Oilers, who joined the NHL in 1979. Hunter's group reportedly offered \$11.5 million to purchase the Blues and have them move to his hometown. That was a big sum at the time. But many people thought Saskatoon was much too small of a market for hockey to survive. Still, Hunter persisted. He managed to get season-ticket commitments from about 18,000 fans and had plans for a new arena. Despite his best efforts, the NHL blocked the transaction. The league's governors voted 15–3 against the bid, which meant that the league had to take over the franchise while trying to find a local buyer. It was a big ordeal at the time. Even Canadian prime minister Pierre Trudeau sent a letter to the NHL on behalf of members of Parliament on both sides of the House of Commons, expressing concern over the league's rejection of the Saskatoon bid.

If the league couldn't find a new owner, the Blues would fold and the players would be dispersed to the other teams in the league through a special draft. Amidst all of this uncertainty, the NHL moved forward with plans for the 1983–84 season, even though, with no idea who would own the team, where it would play or whether it would exist at all, the Blues franchise was stuck in neutral.

The Blues didn't have an owner in place in time for the 1983 entry draft, which took place at the Montreal Forum. I watched the draft with my agent, Larry Kelly. Through all 12 rounds, every time the Blues were supposed to have a pick, they didn't select anyone. They just passed.

"What's going on?" I asked Larry. Neither of us knew.

The team's general manager at the time was Emile Francis. It turned out he wasn't able to do anything because the Blues didn't have an owner. He couldn't draft players, couldn't trade for players and couldn't sign players.

At first, I thought this was a great break for me. They had missed out on an entire draft of players, so I figured that gave me an even better shot at playing a significant role on the team as a rookie. But I quickly realized the situation would have implications for me, too.

That summer, I stayed with my parents back at their small home on Loughborough Lake. I hadn't signed a contract with the Blues yet, and with the team in limbo, I wasn't sure *what* was going to happen. I'd call my agent and ask him if he'd heard anything. Time after time, it was "Nope, nothing." As the summer went on, I grew more and more anxious. Still, my agent had nothing to report.

So it was time for a backup plan. I was eligible to go back and play another season of junior hockey, but that was the last thing I wanted. I had just had a record-breaking point streak and put up 177 points! I was done with junior! I wanted to play pro hockey.

The Blues were eventually bought in late July of 1983 by a group led by Harry Ornest, a Vancouver-born entrepreneur who lived in Beverly Hills, who put $3 million of his own cash into the deal. But when training camp opened up, they still didn't have it together, and I was left hanging without a contract.

I dialed Larry and asked, "What are we going to do?"

"Well," he told me, "we're going to have to go to Düsseldorf."

Peter Lee, a decent NHLer, had recently left North America to play hockey overseas. Lee had been named the Canadian Hockey League player of the year in 1976 and had set an OHL career scoring record of 213 goals during his time with the Ottawa 67's, a mark that stood until John Tavares broke it in 2009. He played several seasons with the Pittsburgh Penguins, but in the summer of 1983 he decided to make the move to Europe. Lee signed with Düsseldorfer EG, a storied club team in the German Ice Hockey League. Larry Mavety knew Peter from his time in Ottawa, and when he found out about the move to Germany, Mavety realized there might be an opportunity for me there, too. In fact, there were lots of

Canadian players over there. If you had a grandparent who was German, you were still able to get a German passport in those days, so a lot of borderline pros took the opportunity. Larry reached out to the team, and they offered me a $50,000 (U.S.) tax-free, year-long contract.

That was *huge* money to a 20-year-old kid from Kingston. And, because it was tax-free, it was even big compared to entry-level NHL deals at the time. It was more than I'd make as a rookie in the NHL.

So I hopped on a plane to Düsseldorf to play hockey in a German league. At least I'd be making some money playing the game I loved. It was better than nothing—and the experience would be *well* worth it. But I didn't sign the contract right away, in case the Blues came through.

When I was announced to the fans before my first intersquad game in Düsseldorf during training camp, they turned on this crazy music and had strobe lights flashing. I was given a puck and a red rose and was told to skate around the ice to the music and throw the puck to fans, and then find a girl to hand the rose to and give her a kiss. Then I was told to sit down in a chair at centre ice while someone spray-painted my name on a giant piece of cardboard and held it up while fans on both sides of the rink went nuts. I remember sitting there, at centre ice, thinking, "What is going on here?" It was just different.

One night, while I was trying to sleep, I heard these loud pops outside. There was a party in the backyard next to where I was staying—and everyone had brought their guns! They were shooting at a target as part of some sort of contest. This was in the middle of a decent-sized city. They acted like it was completely normal to have target practice during a backyard party.

The early '80s in Germany were *so bizarre*.

One thing that was great, though, was the beer gardens. I would go to this one spot with Lee and another Canadian player, Steve McNeil, where they always played Neil Young songs. That's where I practised the only German phrase I learned effectively while I was there: *"Drei pilsner, bitte!"* Three beers, please.

I enjoyed my adventure in Düsseldorf, but I was still hoping to come to terms with St. Louis. Ornest and his group sought to keep the Blues in the city, but they weren't able to get everything settled until late August, which meant they were way behind on the things that an NHL team needs to get done behind the scenes, like ticket sales and player contracts. Even though I was collecting my first pro paycheque from Düsseldorfer EG, I wanted to be back in North America, preparing for my rookie season in the NHL. I'd check in with Larry regularly, hoping that he would have some good news. Meanwhile, the manager of Düsseldorfer EG put pressure on me to sign a year-long contract, which would have bound me to remain with the organization even if the Blues came through. I hadn't agreed to those terms when I came. It was more of a handshake deal.

"Talk to your agent," the manager said, holding a contract. "We want to sign you tomorrow. We've got to make a decision here."

I called Larry, collect, not sure what to do.

"Do not sign anything," he said. "Pack your stuff up and get to the airport now. There'll be a ticket waiting for you to go home."

I pretty much packed up and left right away. The team had provided all of my gear, so I just left it at the rink. I'd only brought over my skates. I had to get Peter Lee to ship them back to me in Canada.

The Blues had hired Ron Caron to be the team's new general manager after Emile Francis went to Hartford. Caron had been with the Montreal Canadiens as director of player personnel during my draft year. Like everyone else, he had the opportunity to draft me then but didn't. He knew I had skill but thought I was too tiny to play. Now I had a chance to prove him wrong.

He and Larry Kelly, my agent, finally agreed to contract terms in late August, and on Friday, August 19, I went down to the Checkerdome and was officially introduced to the press as a member of the St. Louis Blues. Exactly where I'd play that season was still up in the air, but I was over the moon. I wore a velvet blazer, a pink tie and these two-toned dress shoes. My parents came to the press conference with me. It was an incredible moment for us as a family.

As with most contracts back then, the financial details weren't disclosed at the time. But my first NHL contract was a lot different from the kind we are used to seeing today. I signed a three-year deal. The first year, my salary would be $65,000. It would increase to $75,000 and then $80,000 for my third season. I was making $36 a week playing junior, so the money was nothing to sniff at, and I felt incredibly fortunate to get it. At $65,000, I was making more money than both of my parents combined. But it goes to show just how much the economics of the NHL have changed over the past three decades.

The contract was a two-way deal. If I was sent down to the minor leagues, I'd be making $25,000. If I played at least 40 games with St. Louis in my first season, it became a one-way deal—the same salary in the NHL or the minors. Needless to say, I was determined to stay with the big club.

I also received a $20,000 signing bonus (which, I'd quickly learn, was more like $10,000 after taxes). I used the money to buy the white T-top with baby-blue stripes that belonged to my brother-in-law, Neil Belland. I think I had a couple thousand left over after that purchase. It was the first time I'd really made any money. (About a week later, when I got to St. Louis, someone broke into the car and stole the speakers right out of it!)

Later that evening, my family went to a Cardinals baseball game with Ron Caron and the team's new coach, Jacques Demers. Being a huge baseball fan, my dad just soaked it in. And I was in awe at the time. It was all brand new for me. It was hot in St. Louis, so I had changed from my suit into a T-shirt and shorts after the press conference. Demers took one look at my tiny legs and said to my dad, "Oh my God, he's skinny!"

Demers had coached in the WHA and spent a season in the NHL with the Quebec Nordiques, but St. Louis was his first longer-term coaching gig in the NHL. He was only 38 years old at the time. He was an inspiring man. He'd overcome the tragic death of his mother, from leukemia, when he was 16. His own dreams of being a hockey player were dashed when he suffered a severely broken leg at 17. Jacques ended up driving a truck for Coca-Cola while studying computers in college. Eventually, he managed to move into sales for Coke. At the same time, he started coaching hockey, teaching seven-year-olds. Eventually, his remarkable determination pushed him up through the ranks of coaching, all through minor hockey, to junior, and finally to the WHA and NHL. We didn't know it at the time, but later in life he'd reveal that his father—who died when Jacques was 20—had been horribly abusive to him. He also revealed that he was unable to read or write. And yet, despite all that, he accomplished so much.

Players loved Jacques. He was old-school. And he was a players' coach, a motivational guy. He knew how to get the most out of us.

At the baseball game that night, he asked me a question that would become key to my success in the NHL. The Blues had plenty of offence, so if I was going to make the team I had to bring something different to the ice. He wanted to know if I was willing to play the kind of game he needed me to.

"I know you had a lot of points in junior," he said. "But when I see you in training camp, I need you to play in both ends."

"Absolutely," I said.

I wanted to score goals, but if playing a checking role was going to secure my spot on the roster, I was going to do it. All those years that my dad had placed me back on the blue line and had me focus on developing my skills were paying off.

Despite the debacle with ownership and missing an entire draft class, the Blues had a talented roster. Joe Mullen and Brian Sutter were both talented wingers. So were Jorgen Pettersson and Wayne Babych. Looking at the roster, there were a bunch of centremen, which didn't bode well for me. At 27, Bernie Federko was our top scorer and was just reaching the top of his game. Then there were Larry Patey, Blake Dunlop and Alain Lemieux, Mario's older brother. Ron Caron added some more offence by picking up centreman Guy Chouinard from the Calgary Flames. He had played for the Flames since the mid-'70s, when the team was still in Atlanta, and he was the franchise's all-time leader in assists, with 336, and points, with 529.

So before I even arrived, there were six centremen on the roster. But once again, timing was everything. Patey ended up being sidelined with back surgery. And Caron would trade Dunlop to the Red Wings early in the season. Lemieux was just a couple of years older than me, and we were both trying to break into the league. He was a very skilled scorer who showed flashes of what his brother would become.

Through training camp in Regina, I won the approval of our captain, Brian Sutter. In my first exhibition game, which was a really big deal for me, I played on a line with Mike Crombeen and Perry Anderson, and we were tasked with shutting down the L.A. Kings' top line, featuring Marcel Dionne. We managed to shut them down. After the game, Sutter told the *St. Louis Post-Dispatch*: "You're not going to see a better first-year player in the league than him, no doubt about it. When young guys come out of juniors who are goal scorers like that, you don't look at what they can do when they have the puck, because you know they're good with the puck. You watch him, and he's picking up the man, taking the check, giving the check, and going into the corners first and back checking . . . Doug's not going to just score goals."

In the end, Demers kept me on the roster over Lemieux because I was able to play that defensive role on the fourth line.

"You're going to play against the best players," Demers told me. "You have to be the first guy back. You're going to kill penalties. You're not going to be on the power play."

I remember being so excited just to have made the team. Here I was, a 164-pound 20-year-old who had led the OHL in scoring—and I was going to break into the NHL as a defensive specialist, with a key role as a penalty killer. Go figure.

4

KILLER

My career in the NHL didn't exactly get off to a Hall of Fame start. Because of my checking and penalty-killing role with the Blues that first season, in 1983–84, I didn't get many chances to score. My instructions were strictly to shut down opponents. And I didn't get many opportunities on the power play.

I called home often to chat with my dad, looking for some advice while trying to explain the kind of game Jacques Demers wanted me to play. "Well, try to get some points," he said.

"I will," I told him. "But that's not my main thing right now."

It took me 10 games to register a single point in the NHL. Considering the season I'd had in Cornwall the year before, my apparent lack of offence had many people talking. I'd scored 70 goals and had 107 assists, for Christ's sake!

But on October 26, I finally registered an assist on a goal by my linemate Perry Turnbull in a 5–4 loss to the Calgary Flames. And on November 1, I scored my first NHL goal. We were playing the Detroit Red Wings at the newly renamed St. Louis Arena. (It had been known as the Checkerdome, after the checkerboard Ralston Purina logo, when the company owned the team.) The Red Wings had a rookie of their own, an 18-year-old named Steve Yzerman, who had been taken fourth overall out of Peterborough in the 1983 draft. Yzerman scored his fifth goal of the season to put the Red Wings up 1–0 in the first period. My goal came seven minutes into the third period, when a rebound off a shot from the point rolled onto my stick and I tapped it in the net. It wasn't pretty, but it counted!

A few weeks later, I faced one of my biggest tests as a rookie. His name was Wayne Gretzky. And my job was to try to shut the Great One down. Before we played the Edmonton Oilers for the first time that season, I was asked if I was worried about matching up with Wayne. I said no—unless he scored a couple of goals on me in the first period. Let's be honest, there was a good chance that was going to happen. Gretzky was 22 and held the NHL single-season records for goals, assists and points. He had been playing pro hockey for five years and had won three Art Ross Trophies and four Hart Trophies. There was a lot more hardware to come. By the time we met him, 23 games into the season, Gretzky had already scored 28 goals and had 40 assists. At that point, he was on pace for 236 points that season! (He'd actually miss six games and finish with 205.)

I knew I was going to have to play the best game of my life. That was the understatement of the year.

There were more than 17,700 packed into the arena to watch us play against the first-place Oilers. The St. Louis fans were wild. It felt like a playoff game. And we played like it was one. We managed to outgun the Oilers offence by scoring eight goals. The Oilers fought back, but we held them off to win 8–6. It was only their fourth loss of the season, against 19 wins and two ties. But the best part was that I'd succeeded in my mission to keep Gretzky from scoring. He didn't have a single goal in the game, and he had only one shot on net. (He did have five assists. But who's counting?)

Of course, there was no rest for a rookie. Three days after the Oilers came to town, they were followed by the New York Islanders—who, as you'll recall, had just won their fourth straight Stanley Cup.

"Edmonton is a good team, but wait until you see the Islanders," Jacques Demers said about what he called the "perfect hockey club." "They're probably the most balanced team in the NHL."

The Islanders had Denis Potvin, the best defenceman in the game. They had a line—Mike Bossy, Bryan Trottier and Clark Gillies—that was probably the most dangerous in hockey. That "Trio Grande" was my line's responsibility. Before the game, Brian Sutter warned me about waking up "the beast." He meant Gillies. If I got under his skin, Brian said, the whole line would get going, and then the whole team would get going, and then we'd be done for. It was good advice, although I wasn't really sure how to put it into practice. The Islanders scored four goals in the first period, with Gillies tallying a couple of helpers. We managed to come back and finish with a 5–5 draw. So in back-to-back games against the two best teams in the NHL, we looked pretty good and I had held my own—still pushing to stay with the Blues for 40 games to get a full year of my NHL salary.

Rookies rely on good veteran leadership, and I was fortunate to find that with the Blues. One guy who was a huge support for me was Brian Sutter, our captain, whom Demers had me room with on the road. Brian was like a big brother to me. And he would know something about being a brother, given that he was one of seven Sutter boys. Each of them was drafted by an NHL club, and six of them played for NHL teams. Incredible. Brian took care of me on and off the ice. I was just a kid. Brian was about seven years older than me, which seems like a lot when you're 20.

He was the one who gave me the nickname "Killer." Now, I'd really like to say that the name was a reference to the way I played the game—my relentless defence and lethal playmaking ability. But, unfortunately, it was actually a reference to my appearance. I had this big mop of untamed hair at the time. After I took my helmet off, it just kind of went everywhere, uncombed and wild. Brian told me I had wild, crazy eyes. He decided that it made me look like Charles Manson, the American serial killer and cult leader. So he started calling me "Killer." Not the best thing to be named after, eh? But it stuck. So, let's just pretend it was more about the way I played than my resemblance to a deranged serial killer.

Brian's impact on my life went well beyond giving me a nickname and helping me not look like a fool on the ice. He probably saved my life a few times, too. I remember during one of our games in Philadelphia, I was sitting on our bench, staring across at one of the Flyers who looked ancient. Sutter caught me staring at him.

"What are you doing?" he said. "What are you looking at?"

"Who is that guy?" I asked.

"That's Randy Holt," he said. "You do not look at him—he will knock your teeth out; he'll cut your eyes out."

It was only a slight exaggeration. Holt was one of the toughest guys to ever play the game. This would turn out to be his last season. He'd finish his career with 395 games played, four goals—and 1,438 penalty minutes. His single-game record of 67 penalty minutes still holds today.

"Okay," I told Brian, quickly averting my eyes from Holt. It was very good advice.

At the time, I used a curved stick, but Pat Hickey—another veteran, whom I'd kill penalties with—used an almost straight blade. He told me to try his out, and I loved it. I ended up getting a pattern made for myself, and I never went back. Little things like that mattered. I couldn't shoot as hard, but I had more accuracy and I could pass better. These were going to be key features of my game, and it all started with Pat.

While I was learning a lot about how to play at the NHL level on the ice, that first season was a huge learning curve off the ice for me, too. I was 20 years old, living far away from home. I didn't know how to do *anything*. Thankfully, one of my teammates, Rik Wilson, took me under his wing. He was from Kingston and had actually lived near me when we were growing up. Sadly, he passed away a couple of years ago after a brain aneurysm at just 53 years old. I was so lucky to have known him.

Rik played for the Kingston Canadians, where he scored 100 points in a season as a defenceman. He was drafted 12th overall by the Blues in 1980. I was lucky to have a familiar face in St. Louis. Rik showed me around town, picked me up before practices and took me to the rink. He showed me where the best grocery stores were and the best places to grab a quick bite. He took me out to buy some new clothes and decent suits for a fair price, without getting ripped off.

And Rik's help went way beyond the little things. I'd never collected a real paycheque before. Suddenly, I was getting a cheque every two weeks. I didn't know my way around a bank, let alone how to do my taxes or make investments. It was all new to me. He talked me through the process of signing up for an American chequing account, depositing my pay-cheques and applying for a credit card. He showed me how to get American insurance for my car. He showed me who to talk to about my taxes and introduced me to people he trusted with his investments. You take all of these things for granted. I had to learn it all on the fly. The only person I'd ever seen deal with this kind of stuff was my old man, and it wasn't the kind of thing we ever talked about. So I was learning from Rik and everybody else.

I didn't even know where to live. Rik helped me find a small basement apartment, with stairs leading down to my patio and front entrance. I had a small kitchen, a little family room and a bedroom. It cost $300 a month. I didn't know where to get furniture, so Rik helped me out with that, too. But not all of my purchases were sensible. I bought this expensive water-bed that I thought was the greatest thing. They were all the rage back then. You could heat it up and everything. But try sitting up in one of those things after a few cocktails. Good luck! And if you ever planned to move, have fun getting a massive waterbed out of your place. Not easy.

The place was great—that is, until my apartment flooded and most of my new stuff was destroyed. Pretty much all of my furniture was gone. Of course, I didn't know much about home insurance, either. None of my things were covered.

As a rookie, I didn't even know how a regular pay schedule worked. I kept getting these cheques every two weeks, and I thought, "Oh wow, this is great." I thought they would keep coming all year. Then I found out that we only get paid during the regular season, and that's it. You didn't get your regular salary during training camp. In those days, you might have received something like $1,000 for two weeks of camp, and that was it. On the road we'd get maybe $30 a day in meal money. That's not a lot of food for a pro hockey player. On the road, you'd have the money the team gave you and your credit card. So if you went on a two-week road trip, the costs added up fast. The team took care of your pre-game meal, but that was it. So between breakfast, a post-game dinner and a few beers, the cash went pretty quickly. You'd run out of money on some road trips. You had to use your credit card, or borrow $20 off your teammate until you got home. Some of the guys were way better at rationing. They might have had $300 for the trip and still have $150 left over.

I know, for me, there were times when the guys would be going out and I'd say, "No, not tonight," trying to sound like I just wasn't into it, when in reality it was because I didn't have any money. If four or five guys were going to grab a pizza or burger or something, and they asked me to come along, I'd just say, "No, I already ate." I'd know that I only had enough to hit up a small burger shop around the corner from the hotel, so I'd pretend I was just tired, and then I'd go out alone and eat whatever I could. It was always the younger guys on the team who would do this—the guys making smaller salaries and not really experienced at managing their money. Everybody had pride, so a lot of times after a game you would see guys go back to the hotel while everyone else went to a restaurant to eat. Later on, as veterans, we'd notice younger players doing the same thing, and we'd force them to come out and then pick up the tab.

The first few months of my NHL career, I wore the number 18. You didn't have much of a choice as a rookie. I had always worn number 9, but that was Perry Turnbull's number. The number 18 was available, so 18 was what I got. Again, very different times. When Perry was traded to the Montreal Canadiens in 1983, I took his number. The Blues had standard-issue sweaters, a one-size-fits-all kind of deal. But I was only 165 pounds and my shoulder pads might as well have been stitched-together pieces of felt. So the sweater just hung off me, baggy, like I was seven and trying on one of my older brother's sweaters. There was nothing I could do about it, especially as a rookie. So I had to find my own solutions. First, I cut down the length of the sleeves, because otherwise they would hang over my gloves. I couldn't do the same thing for the bottom of the sweater, so my solution was to tuck one side of it into my pants. It was always on the stick side, so I could see the puck when I looked down. Otherwise, I'd lose sight of the puck. I tied a skate lace around my pants like a belt, and I'd pull it tight after tucking the sweater in to make it look shorter. Those were the kind of quirky things I had to have just right when I played.

I also had to have huge gloves. My gloves could not be small or tight, the way a lot of guys like to wear them today. They had to be loose when I was stickhandling. It didn't matter if they were new or not because I'd always have two or three pairs on hand for every game. Halfway through a game, I'd switch them up and put the used pair on the dryer stand in the dressing room. It looked like a big wheel, with an edge, and it blew air up through the spokes.

You've probably heard of the two-finger rule when it comes to chinstraps. Well, I employed the five-finger rule. My chinstrap hung way down beneath my chin, so that the helmet was just sitting on top of my dome. If I got hit, half the time my helmet was coming off. But back in those days, we didn't think about the importance of helmets the way we do now. With the Blues, we usually didn't wear helmets during practice or the morning skates. If we were doing drills, we'd throw a helmet on. And during morning skates, we'd just wear tracksuits, no helmets, and just go out, fire the puck and do a little skate-around. Today, they go out in full gear. That started around 1988 for us. I hated it. Maybe after a long travel day, it'd be great to skate in the morning and get your legs going. But otherwise, it's just a pain.

I continued to prove myself as a solid two-way centre as the 1983–84 season went on, but it wasn't all pretty. We met the Edmonton Oilers at home again in late February, and I was in for a rude awakening when it came to matching up with Wayne Gretzky. I'd been successful once, which meant it was unlikely I'd have the same result again. This time, Gretzky managed to get much more than a single shot. In fact, he scored four goals, including one off a bad giveaway by me. He added two assists for good measure, and the Oilers beat us 6–5. I picked up a goal in the game, but it was little consolation for Gretzky's scoring outburst. It wasn't entirely my fault, but it still stung. And it wouldn't be the last time the Great One beat me.

That season, I also got into one of my first fights in the NHL. Thankfully, it was with my brother-in-law, Neil Belland, who was playing for the Vancouver Canucks at the time. There was a bit of a pileup after a whistle, and everyone on the ice grabbed a partner. I paired up with Neil. We ended up wrestling on the ice, laughing, while the referee and linesmen tried to pull everyone apart.

"Should we tell them we're related?" I asked Neil as they pulled us apart.

It was a non-decision, of course.

The Blues went on to finish second in the weak Norris Division with a 32–41–7 record that season. Still, my rookie campaign had gone as I'd hoped it would. Jacques Demers openly argued that I should be in the running for rookie of the year. But I didn't have the goals and assists of guys like Yzerman and Sylvain Turgeon, who had gone second overall to the Hartford Whalers in the 1983 draft. They'd finish with

87 and 72 points respectively. But after spending my first few months in the league in a mainly defensive role, I still managed to put up 53 points, with 25 goals and 28 assists.

In the end, the Buffalo Sabres' 18-year-old goalie, Tom Barrasso, posted a 2.84 goals-against average and took home the Calder Trophy, along with the Vézina Trophy—becoming only the third goalie to win both in the same year.

The last half of the season, Demers had let me open up offensively, and I was able to produce. "It's a tribute to him that he accepted his defensive role in the first half of the season, and now he's become a complete hockey player," Demers said. I was happy with that, especially because I'd also proven my value as a defensive forward. And I knew the points would come eventually, but I was making my mark in other ways.

We faced the Detroit Red Wings in the first round of the playoffs. My job was to shut Steve Yzerman down. We won the first game 3–2 at home at the Arena but lost the second 5–3 in front of a tepid home crowd of 13,426 fans. It was a violent affair, with 25 penalties and 137 total minutes spent in the sin bin between both teams—74 of those minutes belonged to us, which was a franchise record for a single playoff game. Our next game was at the raucous Joe Louis Arena, where fans were watching a playoff game for the first time since the rink was built in 1979. They packed in 20,000 very loud people. But despite the noise, we managed to squeak out a 4–3 double-overtime win. The next night, I assisted on all three goals—and our goalie, Mike Liut, stopped 40 shots—in our 3–2 win over the Red Wings.

We faced the Minnesota North Stars in the second round, the only team in the "Chuck Norris" Division that finished with a record above .500. We dropped the first game in Minnesota, but I picked up the overtime winner in our 4–3 victory in Game 2. The best-of-seven battle went back and forth, all the way to the seventh game. We were leading 3–2 with just six minutes left in the third period when the North Stars tied it up to force overtime. Then, Steve Payne scored six minutes into the sudden-death overtime to win the series for the North Stars.

It was a disappointing way to go out. But my first NHL season was behind me, and all things considered, it had been a success. I was only a couple months away from my 21st birthday. I was still a kid with a big mop of black hair who weighed just a touch more than a buck sixty.

"He'll gain some weight. He'll get stronger," Demers said at the time. "He has a bright future," he told the *St. Louis Post-Dispatch*.

I went back to St. Louis and went through my locker, getting ready to head home to Kingston, where I would train during the off-season. Throughout my short career, I had always collected my sweaters from each team I played for. Well, it turned out that the Blues wouldn't allow us to keep our sweaters. They were team property and would be reused for training camps and other things. They had only one set each of home and away sweaters. Talk about different times!

Later, I'd find ways to smuggle my sweaters out of the arena and pretend they were lost. But I wasn't that bold as a rookie. So to this day, the only sweater I don't have from my playing days is that number 18 Blues sweater.

Most of the players drove home after the season back then, because flying was too expensive. Mostly, it was back to where we came from, along the road we took to get there. I was looking forward to getting back to my parents and seeing my sisters and brother again. I was looking forward to skating with old teammates. I was looking forward to spending some time on the lake, with family and friends.

As I set out towards Indianapolis and then through Michigan to Ontario, I thought about the year behind me—my first season in the big leagues. I'd made it. But there was so much more to come. I didn't know it then, but soon my life would change in bigger and better ways than I could have imagined.

5
PARENTHOOD

If my life changed dramatically when I first joined the NHL, it soon changed even more. I met my first wife, Robyne, in Cornwall after my last season with the Royals. I was just about to turn pro. She was a nursing student a few years older than me. Things moved very quickly between us. We were married at City Hall in St. Louis during my rookie season and moved into a two-bedroom condo together in my second season with the Blues. Pretty soon, we found out she was pregnant.

If I was developing as a person off the ice, the next few seasons in St. Louis were going to be important to my development *on* the ice. Although my first NHL season had been a success, there were no guarantees. I still had to prove that I was on the road to reaching my potential as a player.

We had a great bunch of guys on our team. We lived and died by the guys in our dressing room. And I wanted to make sure I was doing everything right for them. When you play on a team, you can't have any kind of success by yourself. Everybody on the team is trying to succeed. And the more you work together, the more success you'll have. If you're a selfish player, everybody reads that. It's up to the management and coaching staff to figure that side out. In all my years of playing, I didn't come across many guys that were selfish on the ice. Because if they were, they probably weren't there very long. This is true of any team: if you don't have a good support system, you can't succeed. So, with your linemates, the guys you're playing defence with, the whole team in general: you have to rely on everybody that's on the ice. And how you communicate with your teammates matters. Whether or not you take ownership of your role on the team, and of the mistakes you make in that role, matters. If I saw a guy come off after a bad shift that caused a goal, and he slammed the door or was yelling at his team, I didn't want that guy. It's a game of mistakes. If you're coming off the ice and yelling at a defenceman because he didn't see you open for a pass, the only effect it's going to have is on how your teammates perceive you. Words matter. Body language matters. Character matters. If you come off the ice mad at yourself, trying to figure out what you can do better, that's the kind of player I want on my team. And that's the kind of player I wanted to be.

I was fortunate to learn these lessons when I was a young player, under the guidance of guys like Brian Sutter. We had a great room. Everybody was part of the team. We had a wide range of personalities, but everybody got along. Some guys drank, some didn't—it didn't matter to us. We hung out together, we joked around together, we worked hard together. That's what you want in teammates.

I knew that I had to continue to bide my time, because there were guys in front of me who were better and more experienced. Jacques Demers continued to use me primarily as a defensive forward, even though I'd finished strongly in the scoring department as a rookie. At the time, I would have loved to have been thought of more for my ability to score. But there was so much value in what Demers wanted me to continue becoming defensively. On defence, you *have* to work. You're going against the fast guys. "You're playing against the best," Demers told me. Guys who get 100 points a year, like Marcel Dionne, Dale Hawerchuk, Jari Kurri and Wayne Gretzky. Those guys could make you look very bad very quickly. I had to work hard; I had to play smart. I wasn't going to be the first guy in on a rush, because moments later I would have to be the first guy back. I had to pick and choose when I was going to make a move on offence, because the last thing you want is for your peers and your coach to be disappointed in you. You wanted to be a guy who knew his role and played it well.

I had a slower start that year than I'd hoped, but Demers kept encouraging me. Partway through the year, he put me on a line with Brian Sutter and Greg Paslawski. Sutter had been moved from our "big line," where he'd played with Bernie Federko and Joey Mullen. We were still used primarily as a checking line, but we managed to produce on offence, too. It took us a little while to get going, but by mid-February we were producing like a top line. Greg and I were both young, inexperienced players. We'd both been panicking a little in front of the net, trying to do a little too much and rushing our chances. Brian would talk to us and settle us down. As soon as we took that extra breath, the puck started going in the net. During one stretch in late February, our line put up 15 of the team's last 28 goals. Sutter was the reason. He was the one who got us going. He inspired us. He wanted us to work, and we couldn't let him down.

Despite a strong second half, I finished the season with 21 goals—fewer than in my rookie year—but increased my assists total to 36. With 57 points, I had a few more than the season before, but I still wasn't where I wanted to be as a player. Look, it wasn't bad for a small guy taken 134th overall in the seventh round, but I never expected to play like that guy. I knew there was much more in me. Thankfully, Demers did, too.

He believed in me even when I didn't have a great start to the season. He knew I'd come through.

We were a better all-around team that season, finishing first in the Norris Division with 37 wins and 86 points. We were set to take on the Minnesota North Stars, the team that had knocked us out in seven games in the previous playoffs.

Before the playoffs started, Demers decided to put us through another training camp to make sure we were ready to go. He put us through the rigours of a bag skate. Through a puckless 45-minute practice, Demers had us paired off, pushing a net the length of the ice and back again. Then we did sideboard-to-sideboard sprints across the ice. Our assistant coach, Barclay Plager, skated off partway through the practice to grab a coffee and sit in the stands. I begged our equipment manager, Frankie Burns, for a bottle of water, but Demers denied us any mercy. We endured four more sprints before the practice was done. Or so we thought. Demers had the Zamboni come on to clear the ice and then sent us back out for another 15 minutes of sprints.

Even with all that practice, the North Stars swept us in the first round of the playoffs in three straight games. It was disappointing because we were the better team.

Still, despite the first-round knockout and only a slight increase in points, I had solidified myself as a second-line centre in the NHL, and things were looking up. But there was still much more to come.

Our daughter, Maddison, was born on June 9, 1985, when I was just 22 years old. Maddison was such a beautiful baby. I was so proud to be a parent. It was thrilling to hold her for the first time at the hospital in St. Louis. She was awesome from the start.

Of course, it wasn't all easy. Twenty-two is incredibly young to have a child. That's something I can see much more clearly now that I'm older. Today, I have a son who is about the same age as I was then, and it's hard for me to imagine him being a father so young. I'm sure my own parents were thinking, "What are you doing?"

Any parent knows how difficult it is to care for a newborn, especially your first! It was a learning curve. As a professional hockey player, balancing the responsibilities of being a dad while also being away for weeks at a time was difficult. I wanted to be there for every minute of Maddison's young life, but I couldn't be. But when I was home, it was wonderful. That's when the nature of my career was a blessing—I'd go to work for three hours a day, so the rest of the time spent was quality time with her. Maddison and I would take pre-game naps together. I still had a waterbed. Remember, that was a big novelty at the time! She'd fall asleep on my chest, and it felt like we were floating on a calm sea together.

Being a father grounded me. I wasn't of age to drink in my first year with the Blues, and during my second I couldn't be out at the bars with the boys all the time. Now, don't get me wrong: when we were on the road, I went for a beer with my teammates plenty of times. But the growing-up stage had to come a lot quicker for me than it would have otherwise, and I'm grateful for that.

Having a family of my own meant so much to me. I remained incredibly close to my parents and siblings during those early seasons in St. Louis. I'd spend as much time with my parents at the lake as I could during the off-season, but the summers always seemed too short. Thankfully, my parents would often come out to St. Louis to watch my games and visit their granddaughter. My dad and I remained very close. I called home often.

Our place at the lake still had a party line, used by all the neighbours. There was an old rotary phone on the wall. If it gave off two quick rings, we knew the call was for us, but if it was just one ring, it was for the next-door neighbour. You could only really talk for about 10 minutes at a time. When I was a teenager living there, I'd often pick up the phone to make a call and one of the neighbours would be on the line—"Oh, sorry!"—and I'd just have to wait and try again. So I'd call my parents all the time from St. Louis, or they'd wait their turn and call me. Dad always had advice for how I could improve my game. He'd catch my games on the radio or TV, and he'd tell me exactly what *he thought* I needed to do. He'd be like that throughout my career.

6

SO CLOSE

In my third season with the Blues, 1985–86, I finished with 53 points, slightly down from the previous year. I maintained my focus on defensive play while once again showing that I could produce on offence.

We faced the North Stars in the first round, the team that had knocked us out of the previous two playoffs. In the first game, I was moved up to the first line between Brian Sutter and Bernie Federko, who was moved to right wing. In the third period of the opening game in Minnesota, we were killing a penalty when I stole the puck from Kent Nilsson at centre ice, creating a two-man breakaway with Rick Meagher, whose pass I tapped into the net. The short-handed goal gave us a

2–1 lead and ended up being the game winner. But being up a single game on the North Stars didn't mean much. We lost the next game 6–2, won the third game and lost the fourth—which brought us to a final, do-or-die match in the best-of-five first round.

The Toronto Maple Leafs had already shocked the Chicago Blackhawks with a three-game sweep in the first round and were waiting to meet the winner of our series. At the airport on Monday, the day before that final game in Minnesota, we were each handed a piece of paper, an itinerary, on which Demers had laid out his plan for us in no uncertain terms. Across the top was written, "Absolutely no question that we will be playing Toronto on Friday." The itinerary went on to outline our week, including an off-day on Wednesday, a practice on Thursday, and Game 1 of the Norris Division final against Toronto on Friday. Game 2 would go Sunday, it said. At the bottom, it said: "Do not make any other plans!—Jacques Demers."

Message delivered, and message received. We won that final game 6–3 to finally knock out the North Stars. Greg Millen stopped 35 shots. Greg Paslawski scored three goals and had two assists, playing next to me and Eddy Beers. Meanwhile, I tallied five assists, which was a club playoff record. It was one of the biggest games of my life, and I'd look back on it as a sort of coming-out party for me offensively. During the game, I'd also been hammered into the boards by Keith Acton and tough guy Willi Plett at the same time. I crumpled to the ice.

It hurt like hell. But I picked myself up, gave them both a big grin and winked. That got to them. A good wink works every time.

With the North Stars behind us, we faced the Leafs. After several mediocre seasons, the Leafs had suddenly put together an impressive run in the playoffs despite finishing fourth in the Norris. They were led by captain Rick Vaive and had guys like Miroslav Frycer and Tom Fergus. They had a 22-year-old Steve Thomas and a 20-year-old Russ Courtnall, as well as a 19-year-old rookie named Wendel Clark, who had just put up 45 points and 227 penalty minutes in 66 games.

We trailed two games to one heading into Game 4. I helped break a 2–2 draw by slipping the puck between Borje Salming's skates, then cutting the other way as he turned. I snapped a shot that hit Salming's stick as he twisted, and the puck hopped up in the air and dropped into the net behind Ken Wregget, who stretched for it in vain. It was a nice beginning, with an odd finish—but it counted! "Sometimes you get lucky," I said after our 7–4 win at Maple Leaf Gardens.

That brought the series back home to St. Louis for Game 5, where we won 4–3 in overtime. In Game 6, back in Toronto, with a chance to win the series, I scored two goals in the slot on passes from behind the net from Federko, but we fell 5–3.

More than 18,000 fans packed into the Arena for Game 7. The game was tied 1–1 in the third period, until Kevin LaVallee scored the winner for us with just 13 minutes to go. Greg

Millen stopped 32 of the 33 shots he faced in the game. He raised his arms in victory as our crowd shouted out the final seconds of our 2–1 win. Afterwards, Demers butted out a 12-inch cigar we'd given him to celebrate and spent four minutes talking about what the Leafs had accomplished before he even mentioned us. This was a team that, with 25 regular-season wins, had the second-worst record for any team that made the playoffs. We finished only one spot ahead of them in the Norris, but we had 26 more points.

"I hope the Toronto Maple Leafs, who have not had a lot of respect the past few years, will attain a lot of it after this," Demers told the *St. Louis Post-Dispatch*. "They were the underdogs, but they played like champions . . . They gave us everything we could handle and more. That is the team of the future."

More on that last point later.

Through two series, I had 16 points, which was second in playoff scoring only to Gretzky, whose Edmonton Oilers had just been knocked out of the playoffs by their Alberta rivals, the Calgary Flames. I was happy to be playing well when it mattered most, but I also felt great for our veteran guys like Federko, Sutter and Rob Ramage, who had never been this far in the playoffs before. Unfortunately, Sutter was injured through much of the playoffs, but this success belonged to him as much as any of us. And he was getting back at just the right time. We were in the Campbell Conference finals, just a series win away from playing for the Stanley Cup. I couldn't believe it. We were a good team, but not a great team. We'd overachieved. Making it this far was a significant accomplishment for us. The franchise had advanced farther than it had in 16 seasons, when it made it to the final three years in a row from 1968 to '70. But of course, we didn't think about that at the time. In our minds, from our perspective, the Stanley Cup was within reach.

Unfortunately, the Flames felt the same way. They were led by Lanny McDonald, Dan Quinn and Hakan Loob. My old teammate Joe Mullen had been traded to Calgary earlier in the season. Al MacInnis and Jamie Macoun were on the blue line. A rookie named Mike Vernon was in net. They were a good team on the way to being even better—the beginnings of a potential dynasty that general manager Cliff Fletcher was piecing together.

We pulled out a 3–2 win in the first game of the conference final in Calgary but were dismantled 8–2 in Game 2. We split the next two games in St. Louis and then returned to Calgary to lose Game 5. We were down 3–2 in the series, facing elimination as we headed back to St. Louis for Game 6.

It would become known as the Monday Night Miracle. We were trailing the Flames 5–2 with 13 minutes remaining in the third period when we finally struck back. That's when Doug Wickenheiser scored to make it 5–3. He'd missed most of the season recovering from a knee injury he sustained when he was struck by a car in St. Louis. It was the spark we needed. Our old teammate Joe Mullen put the Flames up by three again a short while later, threatening to deflate us. But that's when the line of Paslawski, Sutter and me took off. First, Sutter scored on a shot that deflected past Vernon. A short while later, with time ticking away, Paslawski scored to make it a one-goal game. Then he stole the puck off Jamie Macoun and put in the tying goal with just over a minute to play. We were still alive. The Arena went nuts. It was incredible.

Eight minutes into overtime, Vernon stopped a shot by Mark Hunter, and the rebound went right to Wickenheiser, who was trailing. He slid it into the net. Game over. We'd survived. It was a miracle win, setting up our third do-or-die game of the playoffs. This time, a chance to play for the Stanley Cup was on the line.

Before the game, Demers addressed the room with one of my all-time favourite pre-game speeches. Right before we went on the ice, he offered one last piece of wisdom.

"They're over there, trying to figure out what we're doing," Demers said. "*We* don't even know what we're doing. Let's go!"

Great speech.

But it just wasn't meant to be. The Flames came out strong on home ice. Al MacInnis scored on a blistering slapshot six minutes into the game, and then Colin Patterson made it 2–0 early in the second. Meanwhile, we couldn't get anything going on offence. Trailing 2–1 late in the third, we were given a two-man advantage. Near the end of the power play, Lee Norwood fired a shot from the left point. Sutter and I were in front of the net; Vernon fell down and didn't seem to know where the puck was. We jabbed at him in vain, hoping to knock it free. It was that close.

And then it was over.

We were good, but Calgary was better. They went on to lose in the Stanley Cup Final to the Montreal Canadiens, facing a pretty good rookie goaltender named Patrick Roy. But good things were on the way for the Flames. Three years later, they'd get their revenge on Montreal and hoist the Stanley Cup.

I'd never have guessed that I'd be there, too.

7

BOUNCING CHEQUES

It was clear something was up when the cheques started to bounce, but we probably should have gotten the hint earlier, when we were stuck with the job of booking our own flights home from Calgary.

Heading into Game 7 of the conference final in 1986, we were set to take a charter flight from Calgary to Montreal to start the Stanley Cup Final if we came out as the victors. We assumed that the same plane would take us home to St. Louis if we lost. We assumed wrong. When we woke up the morning after losing Game 7, we found out that, at the behest of Harry Ornest, the Blues' owner, management had cancelled the charter. We had to go to the airport and pay our own way back. That was frustrating, particularly for guys on the team who were making relatively small paycheques. I'd just finished the final season of my three-year deal, with an $85,000 salary. But our paycheques stopped coming at the end of the regular season, and we were depending on playoff bonus money that was yet to come. I'm not complaining about my salary, but I had a wife and a baby to take care of, too. It wasn't like money wasn't a concern. My credit card had a limit of a thousand bucks. Booking a last-minute flight from Calgary to Salt Lake City, and then from Salt Lake City to St. Louis, put me right up against it.

It wasn't until I was back in Kingston, training during the off-season, that I realized just how messed up the Blues' finances were. Usually, you'd receive your playoff bonus cheque near the end of June or in mid-July. They would be anywhere from $7,000 to $12,000, depending on how far your team got. So it wasn't an insignificant amount. We were all waiting for our cheques to arrive in the mail. Mine was sent to my home in St. Louis, and I planned to pick it up when I returned partway through the summer. Other guys lived there all year round, so they got their cheques first. And when they started cashing them, some of the cheques bounced. The guys started calling each other to find out what had happened.

Meanwhile, the Blues were heading in a new direction at the top. In June, Demers announced that he was leaving to take over as head coach of the Detroit Red Wings. He was a finalist for the Jack Adams Award as the league's best coach.

And it was reported that he'd made $75,000 with the Blues that season, which was the lowest salary of any head coach in the NHL. He'd verbally agreed to stay with the Blues through the 1988–89 season, but the team hadn't formalized the deal. Detroit offered him a five-year, $1.1 million contract. So it came as no surprise that he took it. And it proved to be a good investment for the Red Wings, who had the worst record in the NHL. Demers would win the Jack Adams Award with Detroit in 1987 and '88.

The Blues brought in 33-year-old Jacques Martin to replace Demers. Martin had been coach of the Canadian junior national team and had led the Guelph Platers to a Memorial Cup.

Later that summer, Ornest sold the franchise to a group of local businessmen led by Michael Shanahan and sold the Arena to the City of St. Louis for $15 million. He walked away from his three-year investment with a tidy profit of $3.4 million on the team and $8.2 million on the Arena.

After three seasons in St. Louis, I was entering my option year, meaning it was time to sign a contract extension. My agent, Larry Kelly, and I weren't very happy with the way things were playing out. Robyne and I were looking to buy a new home in St. Louis, and we wanted to raise our daughter there. But, not knowing where the Blues stood, I called off the real-estate plans. I wanted to put down roots there. I wanted the team to commit to me for the long term. I called a press conference to talk publicly about it in late August, but I cancelled it at the last minute.

The difficult thing about negotiating these contracts was that we players didn't know what everybody else was making. We didn't talk about our salaries in the locker room. It just wasn't something we did. We could assume that our top veteran guys were getting paid well. Bernie Federko and Mike Liut were probably making somewhere around $300,000 annually—but there was no way of knowing for sure. You might have known approximately what they were making, because in those days you'd go to arbitration. But it wasn't at all like it is today. Larry would get as much information as possible from other agents and would know what his other guys were getting, and from that he could make up an argument for what I should earn.

Our GM, Ron Caron, was a phenomenal guy, a very smart guy. We used to call him "Prof." He knew all kinds of weird stats about baseball, football, everything. And he had so much energy. He'd be up in the box, throwing things around when we'd get scored on. He was animated. But he was also an easy guy to deal with. Aside from these contract negotiations, I never had anything to complain about regarding management or ownership those first few years. But this contract negotiation was big for me, and we had to be firm. I was still unsigned in early September. We finally came to a four-year agreement worth $1.3 million. With the deal done, I knew the pressure was on me now. If I didn't make the deal worth the team's while, I'd be the first one gone.

I had just come off a playoff where I emerged offensively. I'd shown what I was capable of. So under Jacques Martin, I continued to expand my offensive ability. It wasn't that Martin changed the way I was used on the team so much as I was growing as a playmaker. After three years in the NHL, it felt like the play started to slow down for me. The same thing had happened in junior. I might have had a second or two to make a play, but it felt like four. Some players will walk into the NHL and make an impact right away. Others might take a year or two. For me, it was three seasons. I was 23 years old and about to have the best season of my career. I could feel it. I could see it. In those first three years, I averaged just over 50 points while matching up against our opponents' top lines. And then, just like that, I would score 105.

During training camp that year, Bernie Federko started telling me it was my year to take over. He'd been the Blues' leading scorer for the past eight seasons, averaging 98 points a year. But he was 30 years old now and knew he wouldn't be able to keep it up much longer. We had tied for the team lead in playoff scoring the previous spring, with 21 points each. When I scored a goal on my first shift in the pre-season, Bernie nudged me on the bench. "We need you this year," he said. "We need you to put the moves on people because nobody has seen you before."

I wanted to prove Bernie right, but to be honest, I was nervous. I have to admit that throughout my career, I was scared before I played. I didn't throw up too often, but it did happen.

It happened to a lot of us. I was never worried about whether my compete level would be there. I was more worried about how well I would play. I knew I was going to get power-play time and kill penalties. But the pressure to produce and not make a mistake was what got to me.

Sometimes your chances were there, your shot was there, your passes were there—but it just wasn't happening. You couldn't produce. That's okay. You can't get frustrated at those moments. If you're mad at yourself, you start trying too hard and nothing is going to happen for you. It's just not going to go your way.

I often went for a long walk before games, just to clear my head. When I got to the rink, instead of thinking about what was in front of me, I'd try to laugh it off and distract myself. Practical jokes were kind of my outlet. While I always looked serious on the ice, I was a clown in the locker room. I tried to keep things light and fun. And that meant practical jokes. We used to use safety pins to poke holes in the bottom of the Styrofoam cups next to the coffee machine, so whenever the coaches filled their cups, coffee would drip out of the bottom onto their shoes. They were good sports.

Jacques Martin didn't get mad too often. When he did, it seemed out of place. One time, he slammed his hand down on a table between periods and his watch flew off. If anyone else did that, like Pat Burns, I'd be shitting my pants. But when Jacques did it, it was kind of funny.

He didn't show a lot of emotion. You knew he cared, but he was never overly animated, just very even-keeled. He studied the game.

He watched VHS tapes of every game and studied our opponents. He was meticulous about things like that. He'd stock his fridge with cans of Coke and sip on them while watching these tapes. So sometimes Greg Millen and I would screw with him by changing around the labels on his tapes. He'd pop in a cassette, planning to watch our game against Toronto, but it'd be us against Chicago. We did that to him a bunch. Other times, we'd sneak into his office and empty out his fridge and hand out his Cokes to the guys coming off the ice. Jacques would go into his office and realize his fridge was empty, and he'd come into the room and all the guys were drinking Coke. Meanwhile, Millen and I would be sitting in the sauna, howling.

Jacques didn't know who was messing with him until he came off the ice early one day. I was standing in the hall, watching the door to make sure no one saw us. As soon as I saw Jacques, I knew it was time to betray my counterpart. I just pretended I was doing something else and didn't warn Greg. Jacques walked in just as Greg had put his office chair on top of his desk. But Jacques was only mad for a few seconds; he had a decent sense of humour.

That season, the Blues brought in Doug MacLean as an assistant coach. And he was one of my favourite targets. I used to fire pucks into his skates during practice when he wasn't looking and make him fall over. We sat beside each other in the locker room.

Jacques always did his best to give rousing speeches before our games, but sometimes he'd stumble. "This is where you separate the men from the boys," he'd say. "Now, let's go, boys!" I'd always have a towel over my head during those speeches, because Greg Millen sat about 10 feet away to my left and Rick Wamsley sat directly across from me, and both would make me crack up with their reactions to Jacques. I'd hide under the towel, like I was focusing on the game, because otherwise I'd be laughing my ass off.

One time, Jacques came into the room and took his jacket off, and he had this short-sleeve dress shirt on, like a bus driver, with a tie. I was sitting next to Doug MacLean.

"He's not actually wearing that today," I said.

"Would you shut up?" MacLean said, hushing me. "We're trying to tell you what's going on."

"No, he's really not wearing it," I said. "That's fucking awful."

I used to put baby powder on my friction tape back then, too, so when one of the coaches wasn't looking I'd tap a little bit of baby powder on their suit. They wouldn't realize until someone would ask them why they were covered in white powder. Sometimes we'd be getting on a plane to fly home, and they'd still have baby powder down the back of their suit jacket. It was great.

But all kidding aside, I owe a lot to Jacques Martin. He brought some big changes to the organization. He put a real focus on our physical fitness when he came in. They started charting our performance on push-ups, weightlifting, grip strength, Wingate anaerobic testing and everything like that. That's when we had guys hitting the sauna extra hard, or driving around with the heat blasting in their cars, wearing garbage bags, trying to sweat off a few extra pounds. Thankfully, I didn't have that problem. I was underweight, if anything.

Martin allowed me to be more creative. Instead of dumping the puck at centre ice, the way Demers had wanted, Martin encouraged me to carry it into the offensive zone. That allowed me to draw in defenders, opening up the ice for my teammates. It made our attack more spontaneous and less planned. It also made it more effective. Martin put me out less often against other teams' top lines, using me in much more of an offensive role. He would also often put me out on the top line alongside Federko, who would move to the wing. And while I still spent a lot of time killing penalties, I also played on our top power-play unit.

After signing my new deal with the Blues, we bought a new house in a little area in the country outside of St. Louis. It was a great place to live. I bought some dirt bikes and would whip around in the fields out there. (The team didn't know I was doing that; it was very much against the rules.) Mark Hunter lived nearby. He threw a Halloween party for the team that year. When he wasn't paying attention, I snuck downstairs and switched off the power to the house—and laughed as he ran around, trying to figure out what was wrong. He was so worried there was something wrong with the place. It was great. It took him way too long to figure out what was going on.

That year, our team antics managed to get some national attention in an unexpected way. I walked into the locker room one morning, and the guys all asked if I had seen David Letterman's show the night before. They were cracking up. I hadn't, because let's be honest, new parents avoid late-night TV if sleep is at all a possibility. "Oh, yeah. You were a piece of work on Letterman last night," one said. *Me?* I had no idea what they were talking about. It turned out that Letterman had Marv Albert of NBC Sports on to show a wacky sports highlight reel. And I'd made it! I was sitting next to Jim Pavese on the bench. We must have just gotten off the ice from a shift because we were both sweating. And I guess, without thinking, I decided I had to blow my nose. Obviously, there was no tissue and we were busy watching the action on the ice. So I leaned over and blew my nose on Jim's sweater. I didn't even remember doing it. The camera caught it without my realizing. It just seemed like a natural thing to do, I guess. Joe didn't seem to notice, or if he did, he didn't seem to mind. "Here's a St. Louis Blues player giving a new meaning to Kleenex." The audience loved it.

I finished the regular season by scoring 30 points in our final 18 games, with 12 goals and 18 assists, and was named NHL player of the month for March. I ended up with 105 points, fifth in overall scoring that season. Of those points, 61 per cent were for tying or go-ahead goals. Only Dale Hawerchuk had a better so-called critical-points ratio, with 63 per cent.

In the final game of the regular season, we faced the Detroit Red Wings, coached by our friend Jacques Demers, in a match that would decide first place in the division. I scored twice in our 3–2 win, stealing the Norris Division from the grips of Detroit. We had a 32–33–15 record—good for a .494 winning percentage. Remember, this was the "Chuck Norris" Division. We were the only division leaders with a sub-.500 record. So we were good, but not great. We played the Toronto Maple Leafs in the first round. They finished fourth in the Norris, and we should have been able to beat them. But Toronto beat us four games to two. The Leafs shut us down on defence and silenced our power play, which had been one of the best in the league. We managed only 19 shots on their net in the final game. I picked up a cross-checking and a delay-of-game penalty in the third period. It was a bitter pill to swallow.

8

TEAM CANADA

In June 1987 I was named to the 37-man Team Canada roster for the 1987 Canada Cup. It was a huge honour. But it also made me think back to the World Junior team that I'd received only a cursory look for. I hadn't forgotten the snub. It still stung. So when I showed up in Montreal for the national team camp that August, I felt I had something to prove. The speculation in the media was that I was still a long shot to make the team. Whenever I was discussed in the press, it usually came with an obligatory mention that I was undersized. But, especially in my last season, I had proven that I was also underappreciated. I viewed the invite in much the same way as that World Junior invite: they invited me, but no one expected me to make the club. Playing in St. Louis meant that a lot of people didn't get to watch you on the ice very often, and playing in the brutal Norris Division meant that any accomplishments were basically ignored. During my breakout season, I hadn't been considered for the Rendez-vous 87 all-star clash against the Soviet Union. I wasn't even one of the 30 finalists under consideration for the team, voted on by fans. So I had lots of motivation. The knock on me was that I didn't have any international experience, but that was only because I had never had the chance.

Don't get me wrong, being invited to the national team camp was a huge honour for me. And I knew that I was going to have to work my ass off to crack this roster. These were the best players in Canada, and as usual, Canada had talent. Centres Wayne Gretzky, Mario Lemieux and Mark Messier were already locks. So I'd be battling for a roster spot against players like Steve Yzerman, Dale Hawerchuk, Kirk Muller, Dave Poulin, and Brent Sutter. If I was going to make the team, it would be as a penalty killer and a grinder—the role I had played through my first three NHL seasons. Earlier that summer, I trained with Doug Jarvis and Kirk Muller back in Kingston, and I didn't go easy on them. I was determined to make the team.

During a press conference announcing Team Canada's camp roster, I had stood in the corner while the media swarmed around the other players. Nobody there wanted to talk to me. My status was clear.

It was up to me. If I didn't play well, I wasn't going to make it. I was the underdog.

We were in Montreal for two weeks of training camp. We had a lot of fun. There were a bunch of young guys there. Wendel Clark, Muller, Hawerchuk and I all sat beside each other, which was great. We had a few adventures away from the rink, too. There was no curfew or anything, because it was just training camp. So we went out and had a good time, getting to know each other. Just getting to spend time with those guys was priceless. I knew Kirk from Kingston and I knew Hawerchuk from Cornwall, but I'd never played with Wendel before. He was only a second-year guy, but we both played in the Norris and had faced off in two straight playoff series. He was a hell of a player. And we really clicked during camp. When Wendel got cut from the camp, I grabbed his hockey pants—his Leafs ones—and signed them: "To Wendel—Best wishes, Claude Lemieux."

He didn't know who did it. He was blaming Muller, Hawerchuk and me. He knew it was one of us, but we wouldn't tell him. Later, when the Blues were playing Toronto, I was watching them warm up at Maple Leaf Gardens. He looked over at me and pointed to his pants, shaking his head. I shrugged and shook my head. "No," I said. "It was Muller."

I made it to the final round of cuts at the Team Canada camp. On the eve of the tournament in late August, the decision still hadn't been made on who the fourth centre would be. Coach Mike Keenan had moved Hawerchuk, Poulin and

Sutter to the wings, which helped keep a position open for me. In the end, I edged out Poulin for a spot on the roster. Gretzky told me later that Keenan had asked him who he thought should get the final spot. He told Keenan that he felt I was better on offence and had more upside defensively. So that was how I made Team Canada. It was because of Gretzky. It was a big deal, not only because Poulin was a great player, but also because he was the captain of the Philadelphia Flyers, the team Keenan coached. Cutting your captain isn't an easy thing to do.

It was surreal to have made Team Canada. I remember taking some photos with Mom and Dad while wearing my Canada sweater—and it was just this incredible, emotional moment. I was so proud to represent my country. And I was grateful to be able to share that moment with them. I still look at those Canada Cup photos of me and Dad together, and it takes me back through the decades. I think of my old minor hockey sweater with the Kingston Canadians, and all the dreams I carried then come rushing back. I was lucky.

But even though I made the Team Canada roster, I didn't get very much ice time in the tournament. It took Claude Lemieux's getting hurt for me to even get an opportunity to get into the lineup. I didn't play against the Americans in the round robin. I sat the entire third period of our 4–1 win over Finland, and I played a single shift in the third period of our 3–3 tie with the Soviet Union in the round robin at Copps Coliseum in Hamilton. But it was such a privilege to wear the sweater. The final series against the Soviets was one of the greatest battles we've ever seen in international hockey. It was best of three, and all three games finished with a score of 6–5. It was thrilling hockey. But I was mostly a cheerleader, watching from the bench.

In the first game, played at the Montreal Forum, we fought back from a 4–1 deficit. It was one of the best comebacks I'd be part of. I scored one of our goals in the third, playing on the ice with Mario Lemieux and Mike Gartner. We tied it up a short time later. Then Gretzky scored with less than three minutes to go in the third to give us a 5–4 lead. But the Soviets tied it up 30 seconds later, and the game went into overtime.

That's when I scored the winning goal—for the Russians. Five and a half minutes into overtime, Alexander Semak took a wrist shot from the point that went off my stick, popped up and went over Grant Fuhr.

In the second game, it was the Soviets' turn to come from behind. We led 3–1 after the first, but they came storming back. Keenan was using me more at this point in the tournament, putting me up on left wing. I picked up a high-sticking penalty in the first but came out of the box to score our second goal of the night.

We led with just over a minute to go in the third, but the Soviets scored to force another overtime, this time with the championship on the line. It's hard to capture the thrilling tension of that game in words. Ten minutes into the second overtime period, Mario Lemieux scored his third goal of the night, assisted by Gretzky—his *fifth* of the night—to win what many consider to be one of the greatest games ever played, 6–5.

Playing against the Soviets was an education. Their puck control was incredible. We were so used to a Canadian system that really stressed dumping the puck in. But these guys never dumped it in. It was all about puck control and possession. They carried it across the blue line, and if they couldn't find an opening, they regrouped and tried again. All of a sudden, they're going this way, then they're going that way—and then they don't go in, and they circle back again. And their players were very strong on the puck. It was all about lower-body strength. It was impossible to move guys like Sergei Makarov and Vladimir Krutov. Even Igor Larionov, who was a smaller player, was hard to move. Just try to get the puck off the KLM Line, as they were known.

At the time, we still hadn't seen many of these guys. This was before they made the move to the NHL. We stayed in the same hotel as them in downtown Hamilton, and although they were being watched by team officials all the time, we managed to hang out with a few of them back at the hotel, including Larionov and Slava Fetisov. They were asking what it was like to play here, and saying that they'd love to come over and play if their country would allow them.

Soon after, in the 1989–90 season, it was those guys who broke the international barrier, leading the way for players from the Soviet Union to come and play in the NHL. Larionov and

Krutov went to Vancouver to play for Pat Quinn's Canucks. Cliff Fletcher brought in Makarov to play for the Calgary Flames. And Fetisov went to Lou Lamoriello's New Jersey Devils. They had such phenomenal skill. They were instrumental in changing the way hockey was played in the NHL.

The final game of the '87 Canada Cup series was another uphill battle for us. Keenan put me back into a checking role, using me less than I'd hoped. We went down 3–0 in the first period at Copps Coliseum but managed to grind our way back. Somehow, we led 5–4 after two periods. When the Soviets tied it up in the third period, it looked as though we were heading to a third straight overtime decision. But with a minute and a half remaining, Gretzky and Lemieux rushed down the ice on a three-on-one, with Larry Murphy trailing. Gretzky slipped the puck to Lemieux, past the Soviet defender, and Lemieux finished off one of the most memorable goals in Team Canada history.

I didn't have any points in that last game, but it was just an amazing feeling to sit on the bench and experience the energy and excitement of the fans. I got my family a box to watch the game from. It was a great feeling to have my parents and everyone on hand, watching me. It was kind of like our Olympics back then. That Canada Cup would be remembered for the incredible play by Gretzky and Lemieux, but the tournament also gave a higher profile to players like Dale Hawerchuk, Normand Rochefort, Doug Crossman and Craig Hartsburg. We'd delivered on the biggest stage. I'd have loved to have played more throughout my six weeks with Team Canada, but it was an experience I'll always cherish. I look back on it as one of the moments in my career that I'm very proud of. I gave the Hall of Fame my Canada Cup sweater, so I only have the photos as keepsakes.

9

CRASHING DOWN

I RETURNED TO the St. Louis Blues after the Canada Cup hoping to build off the success I had had the previous season. I was playing the best hockey of my life. Jacques Martin offered me two weeks off to rest before rejoining the Blues, but I only took 10 days. I wanted to get back on the ice. I had more to prove.

In 1987–88 I played on a line with Greg Paslawski and Brian Sutter, who was returning to the roster healthy after being sidelined by a shoulder injury the season before. I felt great. I had climbed a huge learning curve and felt like I was close to my prime.

But that year would turn out to be one of the most difficult of my life.

When I re-signed with the Blues, I was making very good money for the first time in my career. But I was still only 24 years old. We didn't have the same kind of financial management that players have today. We weren't that financially sophisticated, and we weren't used to making large sums of money. I tried to put money aside to find ways to make it grow. Well, it turned out that I put faith in the wrong people and made some bad mistakes. I trusted a financial guy who had a connection to one of my teammates with about $10,000. I'd check in from time to time and ask how it was going. He'd say, "Oh, we're up $100 this week." It wasn't invested in penny stocks, but it was close. I didn't know. And then Black Monday hit on October 19, 1987. The stock market crashed. Everybody at the rink was talking about it, but I had no idea how it would affect me. Then my financial guy called me up on the Tuesday. The money was gone, he told me.

"What do you mean the money is gone?" I said.

"The market crashed, and you were part of it," he said.

I had no idea what he meant.

"What do you mean?" I said. "Are you paying me back?"

"No," he said. "That's not the way it works, Doug."

Jesus.

So, that was a lesson learned the hard way. And it wasn't the last mistake I'd make. Slowly, as time went on and I was making a bit more money, I looked for people I could bring into my life whom I could trust with that kind of stuff. It was a slow process, but I got there. Still, every year there was someone coming up to me, saying, "Oh, I got a great deal for you." Right. That's what today's athletes, making the kind of money they do, need to watch out for the most.

Meanwhile, on the ice that season, I wasn't playing like myself. There were high expectations for me after my 105-point season—especially from myself. By early December I'd scored 27 points in 25 games, which was good but not on a par with the previous season. And I was minus 19, tying me for the worst plus minus rating in the league. "I don't feel like myself right now," I said. It seemed like a bit of a hangover from playing in the Canada Cup. I spoke with Wayne Cashman about it. The former Bruin, whom I knew from our mutual hometown of Kingston, had played in the 1972 Summit Series. He told me it was normal and that I'd come around. The only way to get out of a slump was hard work. And I had to learn to relax and not put too much pressure on myself.

But my frustration showed on the ice. I picked up a few 10-minute misconducts and penalties for unsportsmanlike conduct in late November. Opponents were trying to get under my skin, and I was letting them. They went out of their way to target me, and I'd lash out. It wasn't that I didn't want to be mad. I always played mad. "The time when I'm out there and I don't get mad, that's the time I won't be playing anymore," I said. But I needed to get even by making them pay on the scoreboard, not by lashing out. The only thing that was keeping me going offensively was playing on the power play. The majority of my goals in those first few months came on the man advantage. At even strength, I wasn't having as much success carrying the puck across the blue line. Opponents were on to me, and after my breakout year they were more prepared to shut me down. At the other end, I was worrying too much about my offence to play the defence that I had built my early career on.

We were hovering near the bottom of the Norris Division in mid-December, desperately needing something to turn our season around. Things picked up through December. I scored two goals in a win over Minnesota and then had another two goals and added two assists in a 7–5 win in Boston just before Christmas. The *St. Louis Post-Dispatch* declared, "Old Killer is back."

I was relaxed and confident and feeling great. Then came the New Year—and I ended up with a headache that lasted a month.

We played the Red Wings in Detroit on New Year's Eve and flew back right after the game. I got off the plane in St. Louis and got into the little Mercedes 240 diesel that I had left at the airport. On the way home, I drove through a flashing yellow light at an intersection, but when I looked to the side, I saw a car coming the other way, headed right at me. It wasn't slowing down. I swerved away from it and stepped on the gas to speed out of the intersection—and smashed into a parked car. I wasn't wearing a seat belt. My head hit the windshield and my body slammed into the steering wheel. My face was pretty beat up, swollen lip and all. It looked like I'd been in a fight. The cops and an ambulance arrived at the scene. They didn't think I needed to go to the hospital, so they took a statement at the station and the officer drove me home. They didn't catch the licence plate of the other car that ran through the intersection.

I went out to practice a couple days later, and it felt like I was hungover. My eyes were glassy. I was playing left wing at the time. Ahead of our next game, I told my linemates, Tony Hrkac and Todd Ewen, "Whatever you do, don't pass me the puck." That's how I felt. I played three games like that. The hangover didn't go away. That's when Ron Caron refused to let me play until I went in for a scan. It turned out that my brain was bruised; I'd suffered a really bad concussion colliding with the windshield. The doctor said that if I had been hit again on the ice, it could have been fatal.

We didn't really know about concussions in those days. The mentality was that I could just take a couple of Aspirin and keep playing. I didn't even think about how serious it could be until I spoke with the doctor.

The Blues told the press I had sustained a concussion during our game against Detroit, the last game I played before I went and had the scan done. Caron told reporters the injury happened when Lee Norwood cross-checked me and I fell like a "sack of flour." That certainly didn't help my concussion from the car accident.

I was out nearly three weeks and missed seven games because of the injury. We rebounded as a team when I returned, winning eight of the next 10 games—but it was still a struggle. We finished the season by winning just three of our final 10 games, which left us second in the Norris with a 34–38–8 record. I finished the regular season with 36 goals and 50 assists. With 86 points in 72 games, it was still enough to suggest that I was pushing towards my prime, but well short of the success I had the previous season. Nineteen of my goals were on the power play, which was a franchise record.

We beat the Chicago Blackhawks four games to one in the first round of the playoffs, before we met the Detroit Red Wings in the second round. The Red Wings, coached by Jacques Demers, had finished first in the Norris with 93 points. Demers would win his second straight Jack Adams Award as coach of the year for his success with the team. His Red Wings had our number that year. They beat us in five games—the last of which, as it turned out, marked the last time I'd wear number 9 for the St. Louis Blues.

During the 1988 off-season, my name started to appear in trade rumours for the first time. The Blues were moving in a new direction. They had fired Jacques Martin after two seasons. My good friend Brian Sutter had retired at the end of the season and had been selected to take over as the team's coach that year. Meanwhile, the team was looking to shore up the blue line with a veteran defenceman. At the NHL draft, there were rumours that the Hartford Whalers and New York Rangers were interested in making a deal for me. But a trade wouldn't come until just before the next NHL season began, when I was facing the most difficult time in my life.

In August 1988, I faced false accusations, which did incredible harm to my family. It was crushing.

In the process of dealing with the accusations, I was traded to the Calgary Flames. The trade sent me and Mark Hunter, along with Steve Bozek and Mike Dark, to Calgary for Mike Bullard, Craig Coxe and Tim Corkery.

"I didn't want to leave St. Louis," I said, at a very emotional news conference after the trade. "From what has happened the past week, on our part and on the St. Louis Blues' part, it was our best solution."

The accusations eventually went to a grand jury, which rejected them. There were never any criminal charges.

I've long since moved on from that difficult time in my life.

10

CHASING STANLEY

WHEN I ARRIVED in Calgary, there was still so much to deal with off the ice, but I found some refuge in the game I love.

Cliff Fletcher, the Flames' general manager, was in the midst of assembling a potential dynasty in Calgary. The team was led by the legendary Lanny McDonald (who wore number 9, which prompted me to switch to number 39) and had boat loads of talent. I'd play on a line with Joe Mullen, my old Blues teammate, and Colin Patterson. We had Gary Suter, Joe Nieuwendyk, Hakan Loob and Gary Roberts, to name just a few. Al MacInnis led a solid defence corps that included Jamie Macoun, Brad McCrimmon, Rob Ramage, Dana Murzyn and Ric Nattress. And we had Mike Vernon in goal.

The Flames had won the Presidents' Trophy in 1987–88, finishing first overall in the NHL with 105 points. But they were swept in the Smythe Division final by the Oilers, in what would be Wayne Gretzky's last season in Edmonton. It was a bitter defeat for the Flames, who then watched their Alberta rivals go on to win their fourth Stanley Cup in five years.

The Flames were a team that was built to win a championship. And they had had the valuable experience of losing. They expected to play for the Cup, and I was excited to play for a contender.

And it was a great group to be part of. We got along right away and had a ton of fun off the ice. When we were on the road, we usually didn't hire a charter flight that left right after the games. We'd often stay overnight, and we'd go out for beers and meals together. In the hotels we stayed at, we often had rooms that adjoined, with a door connecting them, so we always hung out in each others' rooms, having a couple beers, too. Sometimes full-on wrestling matches would break out.

I roomed with Tim Hunter that first year. Tim was a veteran: a fierce, defensive player who was an excellent penalty killer—not the kind of guy you wanted to mess with. He was a mean guy to play against. He was probably six foot two and he weighed only 195 pounds, but he fought everybody. He was in such great condition that he could outlast people. During one of our road trips, Joe Mullen and Jim Peplinski came into the room. Tim was lying in the bed. He had this big, pointy nose that looked like a shark's head. Amazingly, it had never been broken. So Peplinski looked over at him and said, "Who's the shark in the bed?" From then on, Tim's nickname was Sharky. Thankfully, he was a good sport and didn't take any of us to task for gifting it to him.

Our coach was Terry Crisp, who had played with the Blues in the early 1970s before being traded to the Philadelphia Flyers, where he was part of the infamous Broad Street Bullies. Crisp was a tough, old-school coach. He had a defence-first mentality, which pushed us to be one of the stingiest teams in the league despite having a roster loaded with offensive firepower. He was one of those coaches who was always yelling and screaming in your ear—and I'd just block it out. But we loved Crispy. He was a fun coach. He was intense in his own way. Yelling and screaming was just his style. All the guys that were there before me blocked him out, too. They told me when I got there, "Don't even worry about it." He wasn't going to bench you or anything. But he would say things that were just off the charts.

I'll never forget this one game when we were down a goal, trying to get an extra attacker on the ice late in the game, and Crisp couldn't make up his mind about when to call Vernon out of his net. Vernon made a move towards the bench, and Crisp started yelling at him to stay in his net—and then he and Vernon started yelling at each other. We didn't even know who was up next because our coach was yelling at our goalie. And then Vernon flipped him off with his blocker. It was funny because Vernon was a pretty relaxed goalie. I mean, let's be honest: goalies are, for the most part, very weird. There are some you can talk to before games, and some you absolutely can't talk to. It was just the way they focused or prepared. Vernon was the kind of goalie who would chat away before he played. He'd laugh and have fun and be making conversation. But here was our relaxed goalie and intense coach going at it. It was great!

Crisp also fancied himself a cowboy. At the time, if you got a hat trick on our team, you were given a pair of cowboy boots. One game, I had two goals and was sitting on the bench, itching for a third. "If you go back out there and get a hat trick, you get the boots," Crisp told me. "Deal," I said, though I never wanted the cowboy boots. I went out and finished off the hat trick and gave the boots to Crisp. (It's his favourite story. He lives in Nashville now and says he still has them.)

Under Crisp, I continued to be used heavily on both the power-play and penalty-killing units. I was prepared mentally during the season, despite what was going on beyond the rink. Amidst the looming accusations, I faced catcalls and heckling from fans in visiting rinks and the odd comment from opponents looking to get under my skin, but despite it all I stuck to my game and managed to produce. I knew the allegations were untrue, and that's all that mattered. People would think what they wanted to think. I'd have to wait for the legal process to play out; in the meantime, all I could do was play the best hockey I was capable of.

...

We were the clear favourites to win the Smythe Division, and as the season went on we surged towards another Presidents' Trophy win. A 20-year-old rookie named Theo Fleury, who was tearing the International Hockey League apart, joined us in January. McDonald would score the 1,000th point and 500th goal of his career that season. Nieuwendyk would reach 51 goals, becoming only the third player in NHL history—along with Mike Bossy and Wayne Gretzky—to score more than 50 goals in his first two seasons in the league. Mullen had a 51-goal season. Eight guys on the roster scored 20 or more goals. Meanwhile, Vernon would lead all goalies with 37 wins during the year.

We won eight consecutive games in February to help us secure the NHL's best record. Everything was going great for the team, though in early March, I developed an abscess on the right side of my jaw. It was badly infected and I was sidelined for a couple of weeks. I returned for the last six games of the regular season, in time to get my legs back for the playoffs. We won the Presidents' Trophy with 117 points. And thanks to Crisp's focus on defence, we also had the league's best penalty killers.

Mullen led our team in scoring with 51 goals and 59 assists for 110 points. I tied Hakan Loob for second, with 85. I scored 26 goals and added 59 assists, playing alongside Mullen in 72 games. On top of that, I was plus 45 for the year.

We played the Vancouver Canucks in the first round, a team that finished fourth in the Smythe Division, trailing us in the standings by 43 points. The Canucks, led by 19-year-old rookie Trevor Linden, came out with nothing to lose. It was a rough series, one where we lobbed accusations of cheap play back and forth. We lost the first game in overtime. It was clear the Canucks didn't intend to lie down and let us walk all over them. Gary Suter, one of our best defencemen, suffered a broken jaw in the game, and it proved to be a big blow.

We won the next two games, but Vancouver refused to quit. They beat us in Game 4. We took Game 5, but despite facing elimination, the Canucks took Game 6 and forced a final do-or-die showdown. Had we lost Game 7, it would have been the second-biggest playoff upset in NHL history. (The 1982 Smythe Division semifinal, when the Kings knocked off the Oilers, whom they trailed by 48 points in the regular season, was the biggest upset.)

I was off my game in that first round. While I'd gotten my feet back under me, I think I was still recovering from the time I had missed and the weight I'd lost. The first five games in particular were brutal for me. I was invisible. I was expected to be a playoff performer, but I was terrible in that first series. I couldn't do anything. I tried, but sometimes the harder you try, the worse you are. Sometimes you overwork, and your brain's just not going. You're chasing the puck everywhere, trying so hard to get it, but it's not coming to you. It's frustrating when that happens. There's lots more to the game than skill. There's a mental capacity. Confidence is important. When you're on top, everything is easy. But when you're on the bottom, trying to find your way back, it seems impossible.

We barely won in the end. Game 7 went to sudden-death overtime, tied 3–3, at the Saddledome. That's how close it was to being over. We held the lead three times in the game, but the Canucks were relentless. You could feel the tension in the rink as more than 20,000 fans held their breath. Mike Vernon was incredible, stopping 42 shots. He had to make four huge, season-saving stops in overtime alone. That was the moment I started to feel like myself again. I had more jump in my step; I felt more strength. Then, with just 38 seconds remaining in the edge-of-our-seats overtime period, Jim Peplinski rifled a pass in front of the Vancouver net that bounced off Joel Otto's skate and went in. The Saddledome went crazy. We'd survived, but barely.

I needed to find my game, and fast—because we were set to face Wayne Gretzky and the Los Angeles Kings in the Smythe Division final. It was the Great One's first season in Hollywood, after the shocking trade that moved him from the Oilers dynasty in August 1988. Because the hockey gods are cruel, the Kings had just knocked the Oilers out in the first round of the playoffs, in an emotional seven-game series. Mario Lemieux had led the league in scoring that year with 199 points, but Gretzky, who had 168, edged him out to win the Hart Trophy as the league MVP for the ninth time in a decade. If the Canucks had taken us to the brink, then certainly a team led by the greatest hockey player ever to lace them up would be trouble, too. So, I knew what my assignment was going to be: stop Gretzky.

The first game of the Smythe Division final went to overtime. Vernon made several game-saving stops to get us there. Early in overtime, I took a stick to the face. It caused a good gash, but I played through it with a bandage taped to my right cheek. Nothing was going to get me off the ice. Then, with just under eight minutes to play in the first overtime period, I tipped a pass from Colin Patterson past Kelly Hrudey for the 4–3 win. The crowd at the Saddledome roared just like it had when we finally got rid of the Canucks. It was only my second goal of the playoffs, but it came right when we needed it most. This was the turning point; I could feel it. My confidence was coming back. I was about to be on top again.

After the game, Gretzky offered some kind words about my play. "He's a very underrated player," he said. "He's as good defensively as offensively. He plays hard every shift. That's one of the better trades they made."

We went on to sweep the series against the Kings in four straight games. We were finally clicking, playing like the league's best team again. Our top two lines were flying, and our third and fourth lines were shutting it down. I picked up five goals in the series. In the first round, I had been putting more pressure on myself to be better, and because of that I got worse. I could see that now. As I said before, a lot of the game is mental. The next thing you know, the slate is clean. New series, here we go.

We had just one goal: win the Stanley Cup. But to have a shot at it, we'd have to get through the Chicago Blackhawks in the Campbell Conference final. I had been this far in the playoffs only once before: back in 1986, when the Blues lost in Game 7 of the conference final to the team I now played for. We were so close then; I was determined to not miss out again. Once again, my job was to create offence while also shutting down one of our opponent's top forwards. Against the Blackhawks, that meant our line would match up with Denis Savard, Steve Larmer and Dirk Graham. Savard had 82 points in just 52 games that season; a year earlier, playing in all 80 games, he scored 130.

We didn't see Chicago as much as some other teams. But we knew who they had on their roster, and we knew they were going to come at us hard.

We split the first two games at home before heading to Chicago Stadium, "the Madhouse on Madison," for Game 3. The Stadium was probably the loudest arena in the league. The fans were wild, and in that old rink they were basically right on top of the players. You couldn't hear anything on the ice, the crowd was so loud. Before the opening faceoff, as the roar began to build, I turned around at centre ice and stared back at Mike Vernon in our net. With my back to the Blackhawks, blocking out the crowd, I made eye contact with him and made sure he was ready to go. That first faceoff was so important in a rink like that. This helped me control the pace of things; it put me in control. The Blackhawks coach, Mike Keenan, tried to move Savard around to keep me from matching up with him. But we had guys like Joe Nieuwendyk and Joel Otto who were just as gritty on defence. We went on to win that game in their barn, 5–2. In Game 4, I scored in the second period to tie the score at 1–1, and after a scoreless third period it went into overtime. Al MacInnis ended the game with a slapshot with just under five minutes left in the extra period.

Back home for Game 5, we finished off the Blackhawks with a 3–1 win. Although we were excited to have made it through the first three rounds of the playoffs and qualified for the Stanley Cup Final, the mood in our locker room after the win was subdued. The Clarence Campbell Bowl—the conference championship trophy—sat untouched in the middle of the room. There was no champagne. There was no overwhelming joy. As far as we were concerned, we had only taken the next step in what needed to be done. The last time the Flames had reached the final, in 1986, they had upset the powerhouse Edmonton Oilers in the Campbell Conference final. In that victory over their biggest rival, the team had allowed itself to feel a sense of accomplishment. They went on to lose to the Montreal Canadiens in the final. Not this time. We were proud but not finished.

"We know there's a bigger, better Cup out there," Lanny McDonald said. And that was the only one we wanted.

...

The 1989 Stanley Cup Final was a rematch of the '86 final, but both teams were considerably better this time around. The Montreal Canadiens had finished with 115 points, just two behind us, in the regular season. The Habs had Chris Chelios, Mats Naslund, Bobby Smith, Stéphane Richer and Guy Carbonneau leading a talented roster. In net they had Patrick Roy, who would win his first Vézina Trophy that year. And they had tough veterans like Bob Gainey, Larry Robinson and Rick Green. Brian Skrudland and Mike McPhee were both tough checking forwards.

And they were coached by one of the greatest, Pat Burns.

We'd scored more goals than they had, but they'd allowed fewer. We'd lost only four times at home during the regular season, and two of those losses were to Montreal. Memories of the 1986 final still lingered; 11 of the players on our roster had been on that team. We were set up for a great finish.

We played the first two games of the final at home at the Saddledome, where the fans stood up the entire time. The place was electric. In Game 1, Al MacInnis scored two goals and Theo Fleury added another. Mike Vernon stood on his head the rest of the way and made a huge glove save on a Petr Svoboda slapshot with just over two minutes remaining, helping us sneak away with a big 3–2 victory.

Montreal won the next game 4–2. They eliminated any second chances we might have had on rebounds and locked us down defensively. We hit a few goalposts during a second-period onslaught but didn't have any luck. We went one-for-eight on the power play in the game.

We headed to Montreal with the series split at one game apiece, exactly as it had happened in 1986. The media wondered if the ghosts of our past would haunt us in Montreal. But we didn't care. The guys who were on that team couldn't wait for the opportunity to avenge the loss.

In Game 3, we outshot Montreal 28–17 through three periods and had the lead with less than a minute to go—until Mats Naslund scored with 41 seconds left, to force overtime. It took almost two full periods of overtime to decide a winner. Referee Kerry Fraser called a dubious penalty on Mark Hunter for boarding late in the second overtime, just 10 seconds after he'd missed an open net. Hunter was just stepping back on the ice when, in the midst of a goalmouth scramble, Ryan Walter banged in the puck to win the game with just under two minutes remaining in the second overtime period. That gave the Habs the 4–3 win and a two-games-to-one lead in the series. It was a heated moment. We stayed on the ice, yelling at Fraser, after the game, but there was nothing we could do.

After our loss in Game 3, I got a call from my dad. He and my mother had made the trip down from Kingston to watch me at the Forum. They parked their car in a lot directly across the street. During the game, his car was stolen. The police found it a few days later, completely stripped. The stereo was gone, the wheels, the doors—everything. The next game, he didn't take any chances—he brought his old Buick.

While grand theft auto was occurring outside the rink, the battle was getting even more heated inside. The Canadiens had gotten deep under our skin in that Game 3 loss. It was more than just the bad call. We had sat back and let Montreal control the game. After our pre-game skate before Game 4, I spoke out. As a team leader, I needed to make a statement on and off the ice.

I told the press that karma was going to come back for the Canadiens. I didn't mention any names in the media, but the players knew who they were. "It's going to be a long series," I said. "This is far from over."

We knew it was desperation time. We were angry, but we also needed to get even. This would be a fight for our lives.

We knew they were coming for us in Game 4. We had to be tough but patient. We had to get ahead early and keep the pressure on. We weren't out of it yet. We intended to make it a long series.

"The worst thing we can do is dwell on the past," I said. "It's over and we have to regroup. If we bear down, we can beat them on our power play. We have to keep the pressure on them the whole game. Right now, it's only two games to one. We're not out of it. We're going to make this a long series."

We couldn't afford to go down by two games against a team like Montreal. If we wanted to keep the Stanley Cup within reach, we'd have to do it all.

But any statement needs to be backed up with action. And in hockey, actions often go beyond goals and assists. Predictably, the Canadiens were all over us right from the drop of the puck to begin Game 4. We were outshot 13–3 in the first period. But in the second, I came out of the box after serving a penalty and picked off a pass from Bobby Smith, who didn't see me. On a breakaway, I pulled a quick deke on Roy and snapped the puck top shelf for the first goal of the game. At the other end, I did my best to hound the Canadiens on the penalty kill. In Games 3 and 4, we faced Montreal's power play 14 times without giving up a goal.

We managed to build a 3–1 lead late in the third. With Roy pulled for an extra attacker, Joe Mullen, who scored for us in the second period, missed an empty net. A goal there would've put the game away. Then Rick Green came down the ice and scored with 27 seconds remaining to bring the Habs within one.

We couldn't let them back in.

In those days, it was more common for players to slip in a foot or a spear here and there. I wasn't a dirty player, but I'd dish it out when needed. I tried to get my opponents off their game. There were some guys you just wanted to let sleep (as Sutter had warned me about the Islanders in the early '80s.) But with others, you'd want to get in their heads, because you knew they were going to lose their minds. If I can convince a guy to take a dumb penalty by punching me in the back of the head, then yeah, I'm going to try. Because that takes their focus off of scoring. Instead, they'd be thinking, "Where is that little bastard?" Opponents would be trying to do it to you, too. Thankfully, the TV microphones rarely picked up the stuff we'd say on the ice. There were a lot of things said that were best left between the boards, like heated conversations about a player's mother, sister, wife and so on.

Everybody got into your head sooner or later. But along with your team's game plan, you have to have your own plan for who you're about to face. You have to know who on the other team is going to chirp at you, and who on that team is going to run you. With experience, you become more aware of what's likely to happen, and you also learn how to say something to a guy, or hit him, and then skate away. That pisses people off more than anything.

That's how I approached Claude Lemieux. He was one of the Canadiens I ran up against in that series. He was brutal to play against. And he'd been in Burns's bad books and been benched for the second and third games of the series. He was back in the lineup for Game 4, and he was on the ice when Green scored the Canadiens' second goal. So, as we were skating away from the play, I kicked him in the back of the legs. He spun around and sucker-punched me, right in front of the ref. I fell backwards, hard, with an Oscar-worthy performance. I mean, he connected and I was going down regardless, but I didn't exactly brace myself for my fall. For his trouble, Lemieux took a trip to the box. This is the kind of assist you never get credit for. We held off the Canadiens' attack the rest of the way, and I passed the puck to Mullen for another chance at the empty net with 11 seconds to go. This time, he hit it. We won 4–2.

I was held back to do an interview on live television before leaving the ice. The Canadiens fans hung over the glass, hurling insults at me the entire time. But it didn't matter. We'd tied the series 2–2. We were alive and we were heading home.

Back at the Saddledome for Game 5, more than 20,000 fans once again stood on their feet, willing us towards the team's first Stanley Cup. It was incredible. But as a team, we couldn't afford to get caught up in the emotion and anticipation. We had to play our game. We had to be methodical and break the Canadiens down. It was a best-of-three series now. There was no room for mistakes.

Thankfully, we jumped out to an early first-period lead with goals from Joel Otto, Joe Mullen and Al MacInnis. All we had to do was hang on. And we did, but it was tough. Montreal tried everything they could to get back in the game. They scored two and pushed hard for a tying goal in the third. Crisp double-shifted Otto, Mullen and me through the third period, using our two-way game to temper the Habs' attack. Vernon stood tall in goal, making a big save on Mike Keane with four minutes to go. With Patrick Roy on the bench for an extra attacker, Vernon shut the door again with goalmouth stops on Bobby Smith and Claude Lemieux. We pulled through with a 3–2 win. The Saddle nearly popped off the rink.

We were one game away from lifting the Stanley Cup.

At that point in my career, at just 24 years old, I already knew how difficult it was to get this far in the NHL playoffs. But I couldn't fully comprehend just how rare the experience was.

"Some guys won't have this chance again," I thought when we arrived in Montreal with a chance to claim the Cup in Game 6. Of course, I didn't know then that I was talking about myself.

Throughout the Stanley Cup Final, I had a little superstition that I had to take care of before every game: I'd wait in the hallway outside the locker room for Don Cherry to pass by and I'd shake his hand. I *had* to do it. I guess we had chatted before one of our wins in the series against the Blackhawks, so I figured Don was good luck. We'd been friends for some time, even at that point, because of our Kingston connection. Don also coached my brother, Dave, when he played for the Rochester Americans. Grapes was biased towards me throughout my career, and I'd always appreciate the support (and the on-air kisses).

Before I put my skates on ahead of Game 6, I walked out into the hallway to find him again. I couldn't see him anywhere, so I went on a short mission to figure out where he was. Finally, I spotted him standing by the gate to the ice, so I quickly went over and shook hands with my good luck charm. A photographer was there and managed to snap a photo of it. No one knew what the handshake was about at the time, but that was it. I went back to the locker room and got dressed, knowing that my luck was taken care of.

It worked. Because that night we became the first visiting team to claim a Stanley Cup at the Forum in 68 years.

Once again, Mike Vernon was incredible in net. He held

off a desperate attack from the Habs in the first period, while Colin Patterson scored to put us on the board first. Claude Lemieux scored in the second, but we countered quickly as Nieuwendyk fed a cross-ice pass to Lanny McDonald, who fired in what would be the last goal of his career. We carried a 2–1 lead into the third period. In the final frame, Russ Courtnall collided with Vernon behind our net and was sent to the box. On the power play, I took a pass from Mullen just over the Habs' blue line and cut towards the net. I snapped a backhand shot at Roy, who bobbled the puck. I batted it out of the air into the net as he tried to find it. It was the biggest goal of my career. We were up 3–1. But it wasn't over yet.

With eight minutes left in a wild third period, Rick Green—who had been goalless in the playoffs—took a shot through traffic that found the back of the net. Montreal was within one goal, and the Forum went wild.

Those final eight minutes were a war. I was double-shifting again, trying to shut down any hope the Habs had left. Then, with just over a minute to play and the Montreal net empty, I took a pass from Mullen at centre ice, cut to the wing as I crossed the blue line and shot from the far hash marks at the empty net. I saw it cross the goal line just as I crashed into the boards. I got up and jumped into the arms of Rob Ramage. One minute later, the piercing siren sounded—and we were Stanley Cup champions.

Our captains, Lanny McDonald, Tim Hunter and Jim Peplinski, accepted the Cup from NHL president John Ziegler.

We crowded around together. It was just incredible. Lanny's skate around the Forum with the Cup was an amazing way to cap his career. My teammates passed the Cup around, taking their turns living out boyhood dreams of hoisting the famous trophy. I actually didn't do a lap. We'd already done about 20 around the rink by the time it came to me, and I was exhausted by then. We'd just won and I could barely smile anymore! We were hugging everybody and celebrating. It was overwhelming. You almost just want to get off the ice after the pictures and get into the room to shave the playoff beard off. We took our photo on the ice and carried the trophy into the locker room. That's where I got a chance to sit next to it and let it all sink in.

The best part was that my dad had made his way down to the locker room, along with my mom and a couple of buddies from Kingston. It was an emotional moment. Dad sat beside me while I drank out of the Cup, and then he got a chance to drink out of it, too. It was phenomenal, just getting to share that moment with him after all he'd done for me. It was the best thanks I could give him. I have a picture of that moment that I still often look at today and remember. I'll never forget it.

11

TRADED

I DIDN'T KNOW there was such a thing as a "dancer's break." But when I was hunched over on the barroom floor, holding my foot, I knew that whatever had happened was bad. And that's why my first season as a defending Stanley Cup champion started with a little white lie—and a whole lot of pain.

About a month before we were supposed to head over to Europe for training camp, our friends and their wives went out for the night. Well, while we were dancing, I stumbled and rolled over on my foot. It hurt like hell. I knew right away that it was bad. When I woke up the next morning, my foot was swollen, and the pain was still killing me. I went to get it checked out, and the doctors told me I'd broken a small bone in my foot. They had to put a cast on it.

Shit.

If the team found out I'd managed to injure myself while dancing at a bar, I would be in big trouble.

When I got home, I called up Gary Roberts, who lived a few doors down the street from me.

"You and I were running this morning," I said.

"What are you talking about?" he asked.

"You and I were running this morning," I repeated. "And I hurt my foot."

Roberts got the message.

So I told Cliff Fletcher the story about how I had tripped while running with Roberts and figured I was in the clear. I'd be in a cast for about a month. During one of our media sessions in August, reporters inquired about my injury. They didn't buy my story.

"Come on, tell us the truth," one pushed.

"No, I was running," I swore.

"You know, they call that a dancer's break," she said.

"Oh, really?" I said. My jaw must have hit the floor. That was way too close of a call.

Later, I told reporters that my doctor would only let me ride the bike, so as not to further injure my foot. "See?" I said. "This is what happens when you only run once a year."

That August, we were in the midst of negotiating a new contract with Cliff Fletcher and the Flames. We couldn't file for free agency until we were in our early 30s back then, so we had to negotiate with the team that owned our rights. For the longest time, the process had been so opaque, but in the late '80s we were starting to get a better sense of where everyone else stood. When reports came out about guys who were comparable to you, it made you question what you were actually worth.

"Nobody can negotiate [to be paid on a par] with Gretzky or Lemieux or even Steve Yzerman," I said at the time. "There are other guys in the league, and you can try to make the same as them—except you don't know how much other players are making."

It was kind of a Catch-22. On the one hand, you didn't really want anyone to know what you were making; but on the other, you wanted to know where you stood compared with what everyone else was getting.

We agreed with Fletcher to a new two-year deal with an option on a third, worth a total of $1.4 million. I was happy with the deal, but times were changing rapidly—and before long I'd end up back at the negotiating table.

The cast came off the day before we left for our 18-day training camp trip in Prague, Czechoslovakia, and Leningrad, Kiev and Moscow in the Soviet Union. The Washington Capitals made the trip, too. It was an incredible experience. We played against the Czechoslovak all-star team, and then went to Leningrad—this was a year before the city's name was changed back to Saint Petersburg. The place was in bad shape. We couldn't drink the water because there were concerns about a dangerous parasite. When we showered after practices and games, we had to put tape on our mouths to make sure we didn't accidentally swallow any. We brought over our own cases of drinking water, but we didn't have enough, so we had to ration it. We ended up drinking warm Coke on the benches during our games against the Red Army. Washington had a few extra cases of water, so they eventually gave us some of theirs. We also brought our own pasta and sauce with us because everything was just different there. For breakfast, it was crackers and caviar. Very different. After Leningrad, we went on to Moscow. We played six games in total—two in Czechoslovakia and four in the USSR. It was a wild experience.

Throughout the regular season we defended our championship well, finishing on top of the Smythe Division again with 99 points. Joe Nieuwendyk took over as our leading scorer, with 45 goals and 50 assists for 95 points. I was right behind him with 24 goals and 67 assists, for 91 points. We were still a very well-balanced team. On defence, Al MacInnis had 90 points and Gary Suter had 76. We also added Sergei Makarov, the Russian right winger from the Soviets' famed KLM Line. Fletcher had been instrumental in opening up a bridge for Russian players to join the NHL. Makarov replaced Hakan Loob, who had decided to return to Sweden. He was immovable, and he scored 86 points in his first NHL season. Gary

Roberts and Theo Fleury continued to develop, showing signs of the NHL stars they would become. These were good times in Calgary.

We had a lot of fun, too. Gary Roberts and I were good buddies who trained together in the off-season (which helped make my dancing cover story believable). During one of our games near the end of the season, Roberts and I made a bet to see who could pick up the most penalty minutes in a game. Why not? Roberts was a tough guy, even then. He'd picked up 222 PIM to my 54 that season, but I figured I could take him in a single game if I really tried. But with about five minutes to go in the game, Roberts had me beat by four minutes. We were up about 5–1 or something like that at the time, and I needed to act quickly.

So, during a whistle I skated up to Don Koharski, the referee, and yelled, "Fuck you!"

He had no idea what I was doing. Nothing had happened on the previous play. The cursing came completely out of nowhere.

I repeated myself, with emphasis: "Fuck. You."

"What are you talking about?" Koharski said. "What's your problem?"

It wasn't working, so I skated in close to him. "Fuck you," I said. "I need 10 minutes."

"Seriously?" he asked, incredulous. "Why?"

"Yeah, just give me 10," I said. "I'll tell you later."

"Okay," he said. "That's it—10!"

And away I went, serving my time in the sin bin for

unsportsmanlike conduct. After the game, Roberts just shook his head. He knew exactly what I'd done.

"You fucking asshole," he said. Then he bought me a case of beer.

It was a fun team like that. We were always on each other's cases and playing pranks. We tried to come up with something new every day. One of the crueller gags I'd pull was to steal someone's car keys when they weren't paying attention, and then grind the teeth down on the skate sharpening machine before putting them back in the victim's pocket. When they'd go to start their car, the keys just wouldn't turn over the ignition, and they'd have to call a tow truck. That one was pretty mean but absolutely worth it. The next day, you'd ask, "How's your car running?" And the guy would have no clue how you knew it wasn't working—until it clicked, and he came running after you. It was priceless.

One of my best pranks took a lot of effort and planning. In our training room, there was this hot wax machine that you would dip your hand in if you had a sore wrist. The wax would help with pain. So one day I came in early with a box of doughnuts. I dipped all of the plain ones in the wax machine. And then I squeezed Vaseline into the jelly-filled ones with a little straw. It was a meticulous process. But it paid off. My first victim was one our older trainers who just loved doughnuts. He came in that morning and bit right into one. I made sure I was in the room, getting some work done at the time. As soon as he chomped down, he knew he'd been had. He looked right at me, with wax all over his face, and yelled, "You bastard!" But now he was in on it. All morning, as more staff came in, they'd grab one of the doughnuts and take a bite into the wax or Vaseline. It still makes me laugh.

But some memories from Calgary still bring a tear to my eye. In 1989–90, a family reached out to me and asked if I would come and visit their young daughter, who was in the hospital fighting leukemia. She was a little hockey fan, and they hoped that I might be able to cheer her up. She ended up giving me much more than I could ever give her.

Janel Selby was about the same age as my daughter, Maddison. She was fighting this horrible disease, and yet she still smiled. I was in awe of her. It was incredible. She had such grace and courage. Such joy. She was a spunky little girl. Janel had a huge impact on me. It was a reality check. I knew I could never feel sorry for myself for whatever small thing I was going through anymore. I visited her whenever I could while I was with the Flames.

Janel passed away a few years later. I flew to Calgary to be at her funeral. It was incredibly sad, but I knew I'd gained so much from the enormous spirit she showed in her young life. I'd stay in touch with her parents, Judy and Guy, over the years. And I've never forgotten Janel.

We finished the season with 99 points, still first in the Smythe Division and second overall, but a long way from the 117 we had put up the year before. It was the biggest drop in points by a defending Stanley Cup champion since the Islanders fell by 22 points from 1982 to 1983. So, there were some serious concerns. We were up and down all season. And a rift began to build between Terry Crisp and some of the players.

Meanwhile, I had a slow start. Along with my jogging (dancing) injury, I sliced open my finger while carving a pumpkin in October. I didn't have a good excuse for that one. I wasn't bad through the first half, putting up 38 points, but I could have been better. I picked it up in the second half. In early March, I scored a goal and added three assists in a 5–1 win over Vancouver, which extended a scoring streak I was on to 11 games. I'd scored 20 points in that span. I was feeling good. And I knew our team still had the talent to defend our Stanley Cup.

We faced the Kings in the first round of the playoffs. They had finished fourth in the division, and despite another scoring title for Gretzky, we were the better team. But it was a rough series. We split the first two games at home and then lost two in a row in L.A., including a 12–4 shit-kicking that left me furious at the refs after a series of bad calls. We were down 3–1 in the series, and our frustrations were boiling over. But we never quit. We fought back and took Game 5 at home. Fighting for our playoff lives in Game 6, we pushed the game to the brink, ending up in overtime tied at three. It looked like we had prevailed when I scored with two minutes left in the first overtime period, but referee Denis Morel disallowed the goal. We didn't have replay back then, so there was really no recourse. At first, he said it was because the puck didn't cross the line, but the next day he said he had blown his whistle. Then, Mike Krushelnyski scored for the Kings three minutes into the second overtime period to finish us off.

It was a bitter end. We were the Stanley Cup champions, and now we were gone in the first round of the playoffs. Our flight home to Calgary on the charter that night felt like a funeral. We quickly dispersed after touching down.

Some of us hopped on a flight to Bern, Switzerland, to play for Canada in the world championship. I played on a line with Theo Fleury, and Al MacInnis and Jamie Macoun joined the team, too. It was great to have another opportunity to play for Canada, and we had a lot of fun over there. We had guys like Steve Yzerman, Brian Bellows and Doug Lidster on the team, and Kirk McLean was in net. But we ended up flaming out after the first round, losing all three games in the final round and finishing fourth in the tournament.

Meanwhile, back home, the Flames fired Terry Crisp after our disappointing finish. He was replaced by Doug Risebrough, who had been working as our assistant GM alongside Cliff Fletcher. Risebrough was only 36 years old when he signed a three-year deal to take the reins as head coach, but he had a lot of experience with winning. He'd won four Stanley Cups as a member of the Montreal Canadiens, and he added a fifth ring when he was assistant coach during our win in '89.

That summer, I tried to bulk up, hoping some extra weight would carry me through the season and into a long playoff run. After the world championship I had dropped to 160 pounds. I had the same problem as always; I just couldn't keep the weight on. So I went back to my dad's old philosophy of packing on whatever I could. While I still stayed away from the Ensure and the mashed potatoes, I managed to come to camp 13 pounds heavier than I was the year before.

"And if I just stay on the steroids for two more years, I can keep it on," I joked at the time.

"No . . . I'm eating more. I'm taking lots of protein. As long as we're playing, it's no problem. If you take it and don't do anything, you're just going to get fat. I think it'll make me feel stronger going into the end of the year."

When I met with Risebrough that summer to talk about the season, he told me he wanted me to step into a leadership role with the team. Our captain, Brad McCrimmon, had been traded. And so had my veteran linemate Joe Mullen. Several of us would get the chance to wear the *C* that year. It was totally up to the coaching staff and the general manager. If you were playing well, sometimes you'd get thrown a bone and get to be captain for five or six games. I always considered myself a leader through the way I played the game. This was an important year for our team. We needed to move past our disappointing finish, and my intention was to continue to lead by my play. With Mullen gone, I was going to have to step up and look for scoring opportunities to make up for some of the goals we'd lose without him.

"I don't blame any one person for what happened in the playoffs," I said during training camp. "We all have to look at ourselves. I think the leaders on the team have a lot to prove."

We were slumping by the halfway point of the season. We lost four games in a row leading into the New Year. I'd fallen into a bit of a rut, picking up only two goals in my previous 14 games. But we managed to pull ourselves out of the slump. We'd go on to lead the league in scoring, with 344 goals. Theo Fleury broke out with a 51-goal, 104-point season, just one point ahead of Al MacInnis, who had 75 assists. I finished fourth in team scoring, just behind Nieuwendyk, with 20 goals and 61 assists for 81 points.

In late March, we played against the Los Angeles Kings, whom we were battling for first place in the Smythe Division. They were one point up on us with just a couple of weeks remaining in the season. There was no love lost between us. We still stung from our loss to the Kings in the first round of the 1990 playoffs, and we hadn't beaten them in our previous four meetings. So tensions were already high before the game. And then Gretzky and the Kings dominated us through the first half of the game, leading 8–0 halfway through the second period. It was a humiliating blowout. By that time, it was already a slugfest. In the first period, a skirmish between Joel Otto and Rod Buskas turned into a shoving match, which turned into a fight, which turned into a line brawl near the boards, which turned into a battle that spilled into the benches. In the melee, Kings coach Tom Webster and I exchanged a few pleasantries. He was chirping at me, and I was chirping back. Everybody was involved, tossing insults and punches. In the skirmish, Tom forgot he wasn't a player anymore, and he grabbed my sweater and threw a punch. I shoved back. It wasn't pretty. Doug Risebrough, our coach, jumped into the fray to go after Webster. We ended up scoring four goals later in the game but still lost 8–4. Webster got a four-game suspension for his part, while I was given two. But there were no hard feelings. I knew Tom and liked him. We both apologized to each other afterwards. Sometimes you just lose yourself in the passion of the game.

We finished the regular season second in the Smythe, two points behind the Kings, with 100 points. That meant we faced the Edmonton Oilers in the first round, in another instalment of the Battle of Alberta. It turned out to be an incredible series. Don Cherry called it one of the best he'd ever seen. We split the first two games at the Saddledome but then lost the next two in Edmonton. It was a big 3–1 hole to climb out of. I struggled throughout the series, hiding a bum shoulder. The Oilers were all over me, and I just couldn't get anything going. But in the second half of Game 5, playing beside Fleury, I started to break out. We hadn't played together much in the series, but together we were able to stretch out the Oilers defence. We didn't produce any goals, but we created chances. Grant Fuhr was a pretty damn good goalie, after all.

Sometimes it's all about feel. And I was starting to feel good again. I'd started slow in the playoffs against Vancouver the year we won the Cup, so it was good that I could feel myself getting back over the hump again. Again, it's all about confidence.

Game 6 was played back in the Oilers' barn, a loud, raucous place that helped make the Alberta battles so memorable. We fired 33 shots on Grant Fuhr but could only solve him once in regulation. He made a huge breakaway save on Paul Ranheim late in the third. We went to overtime with the season on the line, tied 1–1, in a game we deserved to win. In overtime, Vernon had to make two doorstep stops on Mark Messier. Then, just under five minutes in, Theo Fleury picked up the puck in our end, skated down the ice and scored one of his memorable goals. We piled onto the ice. We were still alive.

We came out flying at home in Game 7, spurred on by our furious, wild fans. We opened up a 3–0 lead in the first period, with goals from Robert Reichel, Nieuwendyk and Fleury. But we sat back in the second, and the Oilers tied it back up 10 minutes in. We were outshot 13–6 in the period. Early in the third period, Anatoli Semenov pushed the puck past Vernon in a goalmouth scramble, giving the Oilers the lead. We pressed and pressed through that final frame, until finally, with just over two minutes to play, Ron Stern stuffed in a rebound off an Al MacInnis clapper. Once again, we were heading to overtime.

I'll never forget just how intense that environment was. We had great fans in Calgary, and the Saddledome felt like it was going to explode. We were a goal away from moving on to the second round against the Los Angeles Kings and a chance to avenge our loss a season earlier.

But it wasn't meant to be. Seven minutes into overtime, Esa Tikkanen took a shot from the top of the circle that found its way to the back of the net. It was his third of the game. The Saddledome deflated in defeat.

And once again, just like that, we were done.

It was frustrating to go out like that two years in a row. We didn't know then, but this was just the beginning of a long drought in Calgary. After our '89 Cup, the Flames wouldn't win another playoff series until 2004. In that span, they'd miss the playoffs eight times.

It was a damn shame, because we had the makings of something great. We were close to being a dynasty; we were that good. Sure, we hadn't won back-to-back Stanley Cups. But we would've been a very competitive team, for a while, if they had kept everybody there.

But that's just how it went. The money side of the game changed. It was harder to keep guys in Canadian markets than in U.S. cities. So, you didn't know how long you'd have with certain players. Nieuwendyk was traded to Dallas for Jarome Iginla, though that turned into a great move for both organizations. But Calgary just started losing some players: Suter left, Theo Fleury would leave, Gary Roberts would leave.

That summer, in 1991, there was a lot of speculation that I would be traded. The Flames had a stockpile of centres, and I knew I'd have a lot of value on the trade market. At the same time, I knew that I deserved more money than I was getting.

They hadn't told me if I was staying or if they were shopping me around. I wasn't worried either way. As long as I played for a team that wanted me, I was happy. If they didn't want me, it was time to move on.

I had signed a new three-year deal, worth $1.4 million, with Calgary before the 1989–90 season. Doug Risebrough was the assistant general manager and had been involved in that deal. Two years later, in addition to being our coach, he'd also been promoted to general manager. Now I was arguing that I deserved more, and he wanted to go to arbitration.

But the market had changed. It tipped when Brett Hull signed his massive four-year, $8.3 million deal with the St. Louis Blues. So we knew what kind of money was out there. It had taken me five years to get $200,000 a year. We wanted to make sure I was getting paid commensurate to my value in the league. Brett was the player we knew of, so he was the new benchmark. I wasn't a 60-goal scorer, but I was a 90-point guy.

My agent, Larry Kelly, looked at the figures and made an argument for my value based on what similar guys were making. We had arbitration in November of the 1991–92 season. Everything was internal. The media and the public didn't really know what was going on. I had been making $325,000 per year with the Flames, and in front of the arbitrator we argued that I deserved to be making $700,000. I still have the massive binder Larry put together to make the case that I deserved more. It was full of stats and affidavits from other players, like Gretzky, saying that they agreed that I deserved what we were asking for. Larry went through his book with the arbitrator for two hours, page by page, laying out our case.

Meanwhile, Risebrough came in with three pieces of paper stapled together. He got so frustrated that he threw his pamphlet down and huffed, "He doesn't deserve that amount of money!"

The Flames countered our $700,000 figure with $400,000. The arbitrator awarded me $625,000.

Honestly, the whole arbitration process seemed like a joke to me. We'd played the day before the arbitration hearing, and I remember looking up and seeing Risebrough sitting up in his box with someone. After the game was over, I asked my agent who he was with. It was the arbitrator. So I was thinking, "Well, great—how's *this* going to go?"

But I was surprised. At the end of the day, it worked out well for us. We felt we had won.

But a month and a half later, I'd be gone.

We played against San Jose on November 30. I woke up in the hotel that morning to go to the bathroom. I overheard a voice in the other room. It was Risebrough, whose room was right next to mine. He was on the phone. I heard my name. I lay down on the floor beside the door that connected the two rooms and put my ear to the narrow gap at the floor. That's when I heard it.

"I'm going to trade Gilmour."

I knew then that I was finished with the Calgary Flames.

I called Larry. "No, don't do anything," he said. "Just hang in there." He was going to find out what was happening. But I knew then that I was done in Calgary. It was frustrating because you want to be wanted, right? But Risebrough was the coach *and* the GM. There was nothing I could do.

My agent called up Hockey Canada, which was based in Calgary at the time, and asked if there would be a spot for me to train and play with the national team if I wasn't with the Flames. They were pretty confused, not knowing what was going on, but they said there was a spot for me on the team if I wanted it. Team Canada was made up of guys who were trying to get to the pro ranks and guys whose professional careers were done. I was 28 years old and didn't fit into either camp, but I told Larry it might be a good opportunity to be able to continue skating until they moved me.

I waited a month and then decided I wasn't waiting any longer. After the morning skate on New Year's Eve, I prepared my exit. I had about three dozen sticks in my locker at the arena, so I took about a dozen and a half, snuck out the back door and put them in my car. I went home after the skate, had a pre-game nap and came back for the game.

. . .

In what turned out to be my last game as a Flame, I leapt free from a pack of Canadiens players and swept in alone on Patrick Roy to score a short-handed goal. Later, in overtime, I assisted on Paul Ranheim's game-winning goal with a cross-ice pass. We won 3–2.

I was on *Hockey Night in Canada* after the game, chatting with Ron MacLean and Don Cherry. I wasn't really saying anything at all, aside from some clichés about the game. We'd played against Kirk Muller, so I think we were chatting about our Kingston connection. But in the back of my mind, I was thinking about how I was going to clear the rest of my equipment out of the Saddledome in the morning. I was done. In fact, the only person I told was Don Cherry, right after we went off the air. I trusted him. He could have broken the story right there that night, but he didn't. He knew I needed to do it on my own terms and didn't need a firestorm of media after me on New Year's Eve.

We went to a restaurant as a team after the game was over. I was sitting at the table with a small group of the guys I was closest to and the other captains, like Roberts and MacInnis. That's when I told them for the first time.

"Guys, if I'm not there tomorrow, I'm done," I said.

And they were like, "'What? Fuck off!"

"I'm not going back," I said. "I'm done. I know I'm going to get traded. You guys know I'm probably going to get traded. It's not going to work."

They told me to have a drink, cool off and think about it the next day. But I knew what I was doing.

I went in at seven o'clock the next morning and packed up the gear I could use, like my skates and other stuff I was going to need. My gloves and helmet belonged to Calgary, so I left them behind. Paul Baxter, our assistant coach, was there and asked me what I was doing.

"Well, I'm gone today," I said.

Baxter told me that Risebrough was upstairs in his office. I put my equipment in the car and went up to tell him myself.

The table in his office was about 15 feet long, which was good because I probably still had booze on my breath. I'd had a good four hours of sleep after my last night out with the boys. I told Risebrough I was leaving the Flames to go and play for Team Canada. He wasn't happy.

"Well, if you walk today, I'm going to trade you," he said.

"Okay," I said. "Thank you."

And that was it.

The next day, I got a call from Risebrough.

"You've been traded," he said. That was it. He didn't tell me where or for who. "Details are coming."

About an hour later, Rick Wamsley called me. "Have you heard what's going on?" he asked.

"I don't even know where I've been traded to," I said.

"You've been traded to Toronto," Wamsley said. "And there's *a lot* of us going."

12

BLUE AND WHITE

I WALKED OUT of the visiting locker room at the Joe Louis Arena in Detroit and down a dark hallway towards a television broadcast room. The day before, I had been a member of the Calgary Flames. In three hours, I would begin the next chapter of my career. I was handed a blue-and-white sweater, and for the first time, I put it on. A producer sat me in a chair in front of bright lights and cameras.

"Okay, Doug, we want you to be happy, upbeat, positive," the producer said. "And you say, 'Hi, I'm Doug Gilmour of the Toronto Maple Leafs.'"

It made me smile.

"Well," I said, "that's different."

A moment later, the camera was rolling. I looked into the camera and grinned.

"Hi, I'm Doug Gilmour of the Toronto Maple Leafs," I said. "I'm very excited to be here. I've been rumoured to be coming here in a trade and it's finally happened. I'm glad to be a part of it."

It had been a whirlwind 24 hours. After getting the call from Wamsley, I checked in with Larry Kelly and confirmed what had happened.

The media were all over me after I found out about the deal, so I called a quick press conference at my house. They asked me about the decision to walk away from the team. I was honest.

"To be honest, I felt used . . . It's the biggest move I've ever made in my career," I said. "Whether it was right or wrong, I cannot tell you that. But it's something I believe had to be done."

I thanked the incredible fans and the organization, and I meant it. I had been part of a Stanley Cup–winning team in Calgary; nothing could ever take that away from me. We'd be united by that forever. When I spoke to my good friend Gary Roberts, whom I drove to practice with every day, he was in disbelief. Not because I was going; I'd told him it was going to happen. But it seemed like half the team was coming with me. Wamsley was right: there were *a lot* of us.

In fact, it was the biggest trade in NHL history at the time. It was a five-for-five blockbuster swap: Wamsley, Kent Manderville, Ric Nattress, Jamie Macoun (who got the news while at the hospital after the birth of his son) and I were heading to Toronto in exchange for Gary Leeman, Craig Berube, Alexander Godynyuk, Michel Petit and Jeff Reese. On paper, it was a great deal for Toronto and a hopeful one for Calgary. In hindsight, it would look pretty lopsided.

But Toronto wasn't a great team at the time. The Leafs had finished last in the Norris Division the season before and didn't look much better through the first half of the 1991–92 season. But they had a strong cornerstone in Wendel Clark. And Cliff Fletcher had been plucked away from the Flames in the off-season to spearhead a new era. He went to work right away, trading Vincent Damphousse, Luke Richardson, Peter Ing, Scott Thornton, cash and future considerations to Edmonton for Grant Fuhr, Glenn Anderson and Craig Berube. It was a huge deal, and it helped push the Leafs in the right direction. The team had potential.

When the questions from the press turned to Toronto, I was honest. "I know they're not contenders right now," I said, "but they don't have anywhere to go but up. I'm a Leaf now. I'm going to a team that wants me. I'll get some respect there."

I was also excited because I was essentially coming home. Toronto is only three hours down the road from Kingston. This trade was going to be big for my family. It meant my mom and dad were going to get to see all of my home games in person and that I'd get to spend significant time with them again. Even at 28 years old, I had come to recognize just how important and rare that opportunity was.

Leafs coach Tom Watt wanted me to wear number 14—Dave Keon's number for a decade and a half—because he didn't want players wearing high numbers. (It was an old-school thing.) I would have worn Keon's number with great respect. But Godynyuk had worn number 93 before the trade, so it was available now. I liked the idea of flipping my number from Calgary around, symbolic of something new: 39 to 93. It made sense to me. So when Brian Papineau, the head equipment manager for the team, came to me and asked what number I wanted, I said, "93."

"Well, Watt said no more high numbers," he said.

"Well, that's what I want," I said.

And that's the sweater that hung in my stall in the Leafs locker room as I got ready for my first game with Toronto.

I scored on my first shift with the Leafs and then assisted on another, both on power plays, in the first five minutes of the game against the Red Wings. It was a pretty good start, but we went on to lose the game 6–4. It took a few games for us to get going, but through the end of January and early February, we picked up eight wins in 10 games.

Around the same time, I agreed to sign a new four-year deal with the Leafs worth $1 million each season.

In early March, we played the Flames and I returned to Calgary for the first time since the trade. I had scored 36 points in 25 games since joining the Leafs. Meanwhile, the Flames had struggled. The five players they picked up had a combined 17 points since the trade. The team had spiralled to the bottom of the Smythe Division and would miss the playoffs for the first time since 1975. I didn't harbour any ill feelings towards the Flames. It was tough to see my friends have a rough second half.

The only thing that ticked me off after the trade was when Theo Fleury made a comment about it being good that the Flames "have guys that want to be here now." I never said I didn't want to be there. In the end, it was business. It wasn't personal. It wasn't about my feelings towards the team. I'd have done anything for those guys.

I've spoken with Doug Risebrough many times since the trade. There is no animosity. He was a player turned assistant coach, then assistant GM and finally GM—and when you're in negotiations against the little guy you played against, you can see how it's like: "There's no way you're getting that much." Whether the trade was a mistake or not is up for debate. But we've talked about it since, and he said he should have tried to get me to stay. The deal didn't exactly work in Calgary's favour.

My return to the Saddledome was charged. The media made a big deal about my return. I stayed relaxed by playing pranks on my teammates before the game. While Watt was giving us pre-game instructions, I stole rookie Rob Pearson's glove and filled it with water. When he put on the soaked mitt, he blamed Lucien DeBlois.

On the ice, I was excited to battle my old teammates. Evidently, my old friends were happy to see me, too. Fifteen seconds into the first period, my old neighbour, Roberts, and I were both sent to the box for running each other! It was that kind of game. I was double- and triple-shifted all game. And I took my lumps all game. They bashed me around. Joel Otto managed to shut me down until the very end. We trailed the Flames 5–2 late in the third period. With three minutes and 52 seconds left, I assisted on a goal to make it 5–3. Then, in the final minute, I scored in a scramble in front of Vernon—5–4. On the next rush, with Fuhr on the bench, I passed the puck from behind the net, over Vernon's stick and through Nevin Markwart's legs, to "wet mitt" Pearson, who snapped in the tying goal. The game ended in a 5–5 tie.

It was a good return.

Toronto had only 10 wins before Christmas. We finished with 30 and made a push for the playoffs late in the season. I finished with 87 points; 49 of them came in the 40 games I played as a Leaf. I also ended up with a few less front teeth, thanks to a stick in the mouth from Jeremy Roenick. (My toothless grin would become a trademark of my time in Toronto.) The Leafs still ended up at the bottom of the Norris Division with 67 points, but there was plenty of buzz in Toronto about the direction we were heading. We barely missed the playoffs—the Minnesota North Stars were just three points ahead of us. Things were changing. We had quality leaders like Clark, Dave Ellett and Todd Gill, and veterans like Mike Foligno and Mike Krushelnyski who knew how to win. Jamie Macoun was a huge piece in the trade. We also had one of the best goaltenders in the world in Grant Fuhr. And we had a kid named Félix Potvin playing for our farm team in St. John's. We had some great pieces there.

There's a fine line between winning and losing—and I always say that a lot of that has to do with confidence. Once you get back on the winning side, you get a little confidence and you keep on going. We'd read in the paper that the Leafs were going through this long process of change and that it would take years before we were a winner. But I didn't see it that way. I'd just gotten there and it was fresh to me—and I believe we were closer than the press gave us credit for.

Even though we didn't make the playoffs, it was a great time for sports in the city. The Toronto Blue Jays had won their division in 1991 and lost the American League Championship Series to the Minnesota Twins in five games. The Jays were on the way to being winners. As they started the 1992 season, they were the hottest ticket in town. We hadn't had the same success at the Gardens, but the energy was carrying over. We were on our way to something special, too.

When I first came to Toronto, I lived in a hotel for about two weeks before Robyne and Maddison moved from Calgary. And then we rented a place for about four months, in Oakville. After that, we ended up buying a house there. We moved into it in June. And by the end of June, I had moved out.

We were together in Calgary and doing well. Then we moved to Toronto and things just changed. It happens. We basically took a little sabbatical, relationship-wise. I had a place downtown on Wood Street that I had about a four-month lease on at the time. I kept the place because Mom and Dad were always coming down. It made things easier. But I didn't know where the relationship was going to go. When we broke up, I moved into the apartment full time.

I was at a fast-food restaurant with Maddison when I heard that the Leafs had hired Pat Burns as coach. I didn't believe it at first. Pat Burns of the Montreal Canadiens? "Good one," I thought. "No way."

But sure enough, Cliff Fletcher had managed to lure Burns from the Habs, where he had coached for four years. As a rookie coach, Burns had led the Habs to the Stanley Cup Final in '89, in which—thankfully for me and for the Flames—he fell just short. Burns won the Jack Adams Award as coach of the year for his efforts. He'd just led the Habs to a first-place finish in the Adams Division in 1991–92 before being knocked out in the second round of the playoffs. He was up for the Jack Adams Award again, but he had also tendered his resignation to the team.

This was a big deal.

At the press conference to introduce Burns as our new coach, he and I got off to a great start when he forgot my name (perhaps intentionally).

"I don't know the players very well," he said. "There's Darryl Gilmour, and I've always been a Wendel Clark fan."

Darryl? I appreciated his comedy right away. When the press asked me about it, I said, "Tell George I say 'hi.'"

The next day, Burns called me up and told me to meet him at the Gardens. I showed up, thinking we were just going to sit in his office and have a chat. But when I arrived, he said, "We're going for a beer. Let's go."

We jumped in a cab and he took me a few blocks away to Filmores, one of Toronto's oldest strip joints. We sat in the back and had a few beers. After about an hour, some of the patrons started to notice us and came over to congratulate Burns on his new gig and to ask for autographs. We decided it was probably best to get out of there. We went to a small pub around the corner and had a few more beers.

"For us to have success as a team," he said, "we need you to be at your best . . . Practice is everything to me, because it carries over into games. You're one of our best players. You have to be the hardest-working guy in practice."

I loved the guy right away. He was a blue-collar, lunch-pail kind of guy. Work ethic was *everything* for him. He reminded me of my father.

"Pat, yes," I said. "Yes, I will do that."

We talked for several hours and had about a dozen beers. We planned out the '93 Maple Leafs. "I just got here, you just got here," Burns told me. "Let's do this together."

I could barely stand up at the end. I stumbled to a cab and went home.

A new era was about to begin.

13

A NEW ERA

At training camp in September of 1992, Burns was blunt with the team. Everyone was going to have to earn his spot on the roster. There would be no free passes. It started right from the first practice. He wasn't kidding around. If I had a bad practice, he'd give it to me. Burns was hard on you, but at the same time he would also communicate with you pretty well. There was a method to his madness. Just like he'd told me at the strip club, hard work in training camp and in exhibition games would carry over into the season. We had to work every minute that we were on the ice if we were going to win.

As soon as Burns stepped on the ice, he blew his whistle. There was no stretching. It was blue-line-to-blue-line sprints, right away, for about two minutes. Then he'd blow his whistle and give us a 30-second break, and then it was blue-to-blue again for another two minutes. Once that was done, you'd sit in the middle of the ice and stretch. After we stretched with warm bodies, we went on to some drills. If we messed one up, it was board-to-board sprints. Practices with Burns were gruelling and exhausting—just like the season ahead would be. It was what we needed.

Our season opened just as the Blue Jays were surging towards their first World Series championship. The city was electric. We went to a few games that year, and the SkyDome was just crazy. On October 24, the Jays beat the Atlanta Braves in Game 6 to become World Series champions. We played that night at home against the San Jose Sharks. Updates from the game kept flashing up on the scoreboard, and the rink erupted every time. I'd never seen anything like it. We saw how excited the city's fans were, and we talked about it as a team. "Can you imagine what it would be like if we made it to the Stanley Cup Final?" It was an ambitious dream, considering we hadn't made the playoffs the year before. But as I said, things were changing.

It was a snowball effect. It started at the top, with Cliff Fletcher, who knew which pieces we needed to succeed. Then came Pat Burns and the rest of the coaching staff, who knew how to put those parts together and get the most out of us. And finally, it came down to the team. It came down to our willingness to play together, to battle hard and to give everything to win.

Everybody had a role. And that was the biggest thing: getting everybody to accept that role.

It started with our captain, Wendel Clark. My relationship with Clark was great right away. It was easy. You'd play hard against him, but to have him on your team, you realized how strong he was and how tough he was. He was the soul of our team. Clark went through a lot with his body—through fighting, through hitting. He played hard for us. And he needed a lot of maintenance days because of it. He'd be off getting acupuncture all the time.

Clark was our leader. We all followed him.

We had a lot of fun as a team off the ice. We were a close-knit group. We had a lot of team parties, and we went out together a lot. We'd often go to a sports bar next to Maple Leaf Gardens called P.M. Toronto. On a Saturday night, we'd be playing an 8 p.m. game. Bars cut off alcohol sales at 1 a.m. at the time. By the time we'd get over there it would be almost midnight, and we'd only have an hour to drink.

We had our nights. We had a *few* of them. On Mondays, we were at the Phoenix. It had a rock-and-roll vibe. You'd put your jeans and leather coat on. Andy Frost, the radio personality and public-address announcer at our games, was the DJ. On Tuesdays or Wednesdays, we'd be at the Loose Moose. It wasn't every night, but the guys that lived downtown hung out together all the time.

Off the ice, Toronto was great for me. My parents came down for every home game. It was nice to be able to share that time with them. When they were in town, Mom would always walk down Yonge Street to go shopping at the Eaton Centre. My dad would walk with her and then spend the afternoon at a nearby strip club, having some beers and talking with the ex-inmates he knew from the Kingston pen that now worked there as bouncers. Meanwhile, I'd be in my apartment, having a pre-game nap. After a couple of hours, my mom would leave and pick my dad back up at the club, and they'd come back to my place to get ready to go to the game.

On the ice, I was in the midst of one of the best seasons of my career. The reason was simple. In Calgary, I racked up between 80 and 90 points for two years, sharing the wealth with some pretty good centres like Nieuwendyk and Fleury. I was getting ice time, but nowhere near as much as I would get in Toronto. Some games, I killed penalties, but there were nights when I didn't. Some days, I'd be out there for five power plays—and lots of times I was out there for the full two minutes.

It also helped that I somehow managed to avoid missing a bunch of games because of a suspension, due to one of the weirder disciplinary actions in NHL history.

On November 21, 1992, we played the Kings in L.A. I thought Tomas Sandstrom got away with a questionable cross check on Glenn Anderson. I was backchecking, chasing him. My story was that I tried to go for his stick and I broke his wrist. I got two minutes for high-sticking on the play. Sandstrom would be out for about a month and a half.

I was called to a disciplinary hearing at the NHL's head office with Gil Stein, who had taken over as NHL president from John Ziegler. He served less than a year before Gary Bettman came in as the first league commissioner. Cliff Fletcher and I flew there for the hearing, to tell my side of the story. The ruling came down two days later: I was suspended for eight "non-game days" and was fined $30,000. That was the biggest fine they could levy at the time. The "non-game days" meant I wouldn't miss an actual game; I just couldn't skate with the team unless it was the day before a game or on a game day. I'd never heard of anything like that before. I didn't understand it. I wondered what it meant—would I need to find ice to practise on my own? Burns said, "Yeah, you do." He wasn't going to let me just sit at home and relax while "suspended."

They arranged for me to practise with the University of Toronto varsity team on the days I wasn't allowed to be with the Leafs. The guys on that team were just finishing up their semester and they weren't really in full-on practice mode, but the coach promised Burns he'd work me hard. We practised at 2 p.m., with a tough 35-minute session, and then I told the guys I'd take them all out for a beer. We ended up at the Loose Moose. One round turned into a few, and I ended up getting home around 12:30 that morning. These guys were 20 years old; I was 29. They got the better of me that night. I didn't feel very good the next morning. The next day, I went to the rink for our 2 p.m. practice and said, "Thanks, guys, but I'm done. I'm not practising with you guys anymore."

Toronto was the biggest hockey market in Canada, and that meant there were eyes everywhere. When we went out with the guys, we usually had a back room reserved for us. But that didn't stop people from feeling the need to rat us out to management whenever they thought they saw something suspicious—even when they were wrong.

That December, I went to a Christmas party at Originals pub in Leaside the night before one of our games. My parents were staying with me, and I brought them along. I had an 11 o' clock curfew—a Burns rule on the night before a game. We showed up around 8 p.m., and I had hopped in a cab to head home around 10:15.

The next day at our morning skate, Burns got on the ice and came right up to me, close to my face. "So, where were you last night?" he demanded.

I felt no guilt because I hadn't been anywhere. But Burns was an intimidating guy. He'd been a cop before he became a coach, so he knew how to shake someone down.

"I was at a Christmas party with my mom and dad," I said. "Why are you asking? I was home by 10:30 p.m."

He paused for a moment, studying me. "No, I can tell. I don't smell anything on you," he said. "Someone called last night and said you were out until 2 a.m. But I believe you."

Somebody saw me go upstairs at the bar and thought I hadn't left. They called the Leafs' front office to tell on me. That happened quite a bit, actually: "Doug Gilmour was out last night at Bayview and . . ."

Burns's interrogating-cop act was common. He was always questioning us about where we'd been and what we'd been up to. He held us accountable. He could see through us in a way I wouldn't understand until I was much older. He just had that way about him. He knew when his players were ready to go and when they weren't. He was mean and mad before games. And if we had a bad period—boy, would we hear it. He'd point guys out. He'd kick coolers and trash cans. He did that at least twice a month. And I wasn't laughing about it the way I might have been if Jacques Demers, Jacques Martin or Terry Crisp had done the same thing. I was stone-cold silent. Did his motivation tactics work? You can ask other guys on our team, but 100 per cent they did for me.

We'd get fired up after his pre-game charges—"Okay, boys, let's fuckin' get ready to go here!" Or between periods, if we were playing terribly: "Don't let this happen." No matter what we did, the message was that we could be better. We would try that much harder because he told us we weren't prepared to play.

But he was fair, too. If Burns was mad at you, there was a reason. And you could go in and talk to him after games or after a practice. There was no bullshit. He was going to tell you what he thought.

He kept tapes of all the mistakes we made. If he knew you were coming in, Burns would have a list of your mistakes—he'd have somebody counting turnovers, and he *hated* turnovers, especially ones that led to goals. There'd be a big *X* for each turnover on the ice, with your number beside it if you were responsible. And he'd have the video cued up and ready to go. And right away, he'd ask, "What about this play? . . . What about this play? . . . What about this play?" It shut up anybody who went into that office to argue. I can picture him, sitting back in that chair in his office, chomping on the end of a cigar, drinking his coffee and thinking, "Okay, I think I got through to these guys."

He knew when to back off as well. When we were playing well, we were more likely to practise harder. When we hit a rough patch, he'd make sure we went out and grabbed some beers. "Take today off . . . and tomorrow," he'd say. He wanted us to relax, and take our minds off the game, and then come back and work hard. But win or lose, if it looked like we were just dogging it, practice would be extra long.

He was really close with his assistant coaches. Pat, Mike Kitchen and Mike Murphy were three peas in a pod. They hung together all the time, just talking about their coaching philosophy. And they let loose, too. We could tell when they did—Pat would come in for practice the next day and call it early because he was hungover. We always appreciated that.

And scary as he could be, we could also laugh at Burns. I think one of the funniest things I ever witnessed at the old

Maple Leaf Gardens involved Burnsie. We had an old sauna in our locker room that we'd jump into after practice. The coaches' offices were on the other side of the room. One day, Dave Ellett and I had just gotten out of the sauna and were sitting at our stalls in our towels. And along came Burns, trudging along in his towel, about to go for a sauna. A few moments later, as we were getting dressed, Burns came diving out of the sauna, shouting, "Who fucking put that there?!"

On the floor of the sauna, we had a small container of eucalyptus oil, to freshen things up. Well, Burns thought it was water for the steam. So he put the tray on top of the rocks and it burst into flames. He came flying out, thinking he was going to burn the place down. And then he accused us of setting him up! Seeing Burns tumble out in a panicked huff, trying to escape the flames, is still one of my all-time favourite moments.

Over the Christmas holidays, we were struggling to stay out of the Norris Division basement. But after a loss to Detroit on Boxing Day we went on a 7–1–2 run that gave us a firmer grip on a playoff spot. The only loss in that run came at the hands of the Vancouver Canucks, on January 6. Ten minutes into that game, I went into the corner, pursuing the puck, with Trevor Linden. But I tripped and fell hard into the boards, and my head was pinned as I collided with Linden. I was knocked out cold. It was only the second time in my career that I had been knocked out—the first had been in junior, when I was hit so hard that my helmet opened a gash in my head, and I skated to the wrong bench, covered in blood, after picking myself up.

This time, I lay motionless on the ice at the Gardens. Chris Broadhurst, our trainer, rushed out to help me. He helped me to my feet and I staggered off the ice. In the dressing room, Chris asked me what day it was and I wouldn't tell him, because I honestly didn't know.

"I know what day it is," I said. "Leave me alone."

"How are you feeling?" Broadhurst asked.

"Better now," I said. "I'm ready to go back for the second period."

"Doug," he said. "We're going into the third."

I wasn't allowed back on the ice.

Under the concussion protocol that existed back then, I sat out for a game. But I came back in time for our matchup against the Canadiens in Montreal, as Burns faced his old team. I scored two goals in our 5–4 win, which put us just above .500 for the first time in over a month.

A few weeks later, I was selected to my first NHL All-Star Game. It had taken me a decade, but I had finally been included with the league's best. There had been years when I felt I deserved to be there, but I'd been overlooked. I was used to it. I'd evolved from being a checking centre in St. Louis, to a top two-way guy in Calgary, to an offensive force in Toronto. By the all-star break I had 75 points in 53 games and was 10th in league scoring. I was playing the best hockey of my life at the time, and whispers started that I would be considered for the Hart Trophy as the league's most valuable player. But I was also standing out for my defensive play. My old friend

Don Cherry openly campaigned on my behalf on *Hockey Night in Canada*, calling me the "best two-way hockey player in the world." I was flattered, but I wasn't concerned about individual trophies at the time. (Plus, when you have guys like Gretzky and Lemieux in the league, there wasn't much point in hoping.) I didn't have any individual bonuses in my contract. I didn't want them. All I wanted was to see our team win. And together, we were determined to make that happen.

A few days later, Cliff Fletcher helped us out by shaking up our roster in a huge way. He sent Grant Fuhr to the Buffalo Sabres for winger Dave Andreychuk, goaltender Daren Puppa and a first-round draft pick. It was a bold move for Fletcher, who was giving up a Hall of Fame goalie in Fuhr. But Fletcher knew exactly what he was doing. Our rookie goalie, 21-year-old Félix Potvin, had been incredible while sharing the goaltending duties with Fuhr. Despite Potvin's inexperience, Fletcher believed he had a star on his hands. It made Fuhr dispensable, allowing us to pick up Andreychuk, who would be a huge part of our success.

A short while later, the night before a game against the Minnesota North Stars, I was out on a date. I made sure I was inside before the team's 11 p.m. curfew. But it was a fun night, I was enjoying myself—and, well, I didn't go to bed as early as I should have. The next day, I skipped the morning skate, because it was optional. I went to the rink, got my sticks ready and checked over my equipment. Then I skipped my usual pre-game meal at Giorgio's. I went home, had pea soup and a tuna fish sandwich, jumped in the shower and then shut it down for a couple hours. I got up, got washed and walked about 20 seconds from my place to the rink. I got in, got ready—and had six assists that night. I tied a 49-year-old franchise record set by Babe Pratt in 1944. My last assist came off a pass to Dave Ellett, who came over the blue line and cranked in a slapshot. We won 6–1. I didn't know about the record until after the game. None of the guys knew what I'd been up to the night before. I mean, I technically hadn't broken curfew. It just goes to show that sometimes it pays to break with routine.

As a team, we were clicking at the right time. Félix Potvin continued a run that saw him allow just 13 goals in his previous nine starts, giving him a league-leading 2.45 goals-against average.

A week and a half later, we beat the Vancouver Canucks 8–1. I had three assists in the game, which put me at 73 for the season, breaking the team record set by Darryl Sittler in 1978. In the same game, Glenn Anderson collected his 1,000th point. And as a team, we were well into a stretch that saw us go 20–7–3 over our final 30 games of the season.

Throughout it all, we stayed loose and had fun. During one game in Minnesota, Todd Gill and I balanced cups of water on the ledge of the door, hoping to drench the next teammate to walk in. The next person through the door turned out to be Burns, who was all decked out in his suit with his hair combed just so. Gill fell off his chair, he was laughing so hard.

Burns could dish it out, too. Repeatedly, I'd pull on my socks to find the heels cut out of them. It was Burns's handiwork.

The team finished the regular season with a franchise-record 44 wins and 99 points. A bit of a slump near the end of the regular season left us in third place in the Norris, four points behind Detroit and seven behind first-place Chicago.

I finished the regular season with 32 goals, 95 assists and 127 points in 83 games (having missed only the one because of the concussion I sustained against the Canucks.) It was a Leafs record for points in a season, breaking Sittler's mark of 117 set in 1977–78. The team had a ceremony before the last home game of the regular season to congratulate me for breaking the club record. It was a huge moment for me. It was so humbling to stand at centre ice, in front of the Leafs fans at the Gardens, as part of the franchise's rich history.

"I want to thank Toronto . . . the fans," I said over the microphone to the crowd. "We're going to do something for you guys yet."

14

'93

We had a few days off before our first-round series against the Detroit Red Wings started, so Pat Burns sent the team up to Collingwood, a couple hours north of Toronto. He wanted us to get away from the media, clear our heads and get some practices in.

While we were up there, two or three days before we were set to play the first game against Detroit, I learned that my grandfather, Jack, had died. He was my mom's father.

When I was growing up, my grandfather didn't want to be called anything special. It was just "Jack." We'd go to Nanny and Jack's place. And Jack was a joke teller. In the summertime, he'd sit on the deck while my grandmother cut the lawn.

She'd keep running over the lawnmower's power cord, and he'd sit there and say, "Jesus Christ, Nanny! That's the third lawnmower you've run over this year!" Jack was just an old-school guy. They were fun to be with. We used to climb trees in their backyard. We had so many great memories.

Nanny and Jack were both there to see me score my first hat trick when I was with St. Louis. We went to Burger King together before the game, because I wanted to spend some time with them. (I figured it was lucky, but when I tried to eat there again before a game it didn't work.)

It was tough to lose him. It was sudden, unexpected. And I hadn't really experienced death in my life yet. When I was about 12, my dad's father, Grandpa Russel, had died of a stroke. My grandmother, Daisy, was diagnosed with lung cancer about a month and a half later. She died quickly. It's weird how that happens—how two people can live their entire lives together, and then somehow die within a few months of each other. Aside from that, though, death was new to me.

I called Burns and asked if there was any chance I could go home. I figured I could get there and back in time for the first game.

"It's not a good idea," he said. "There's nothing you can do."

I called my parents and told them I couldn't make it to the funeral. But I wanted them to do something for me. I wanted them to pick me up a bunch of Jack's T-shirts. They brought them to our first home game against Detroit.

In those days, we always wore the baby blue full-body underwear beneath our gear. Before that first game, I put one of Jack's T-shirts on over top. I'd wear his T-shirt in every game throughout those playoffs. We were about the same size, so it was a perfect fit. I had three of them: a couple of blue ones and a white one. During those playoffs, I'd sometimes have to change between periods because I'd sweat so much. But each time I did, I pulled Jack's T-shirt back over my head so it was on when I played.

The Red Wings were a good team. They'd won 47 games—three more than us—and scored a league-leading 369 goals. They were led by Steve Yzerman, with 58 goals and 137 points, but they also had Dino Ciccarelli (97 points) and Sergei Fedorov (with 87). On the blue line, they had Paul Coffey, 22-year-old Nicklas Lidstrom, Mark Howe and Vladimir Konstantinov. To protect all that talent, they had Bob Probert.

Detroit beat us handily in the first two games in the Joe Louis Arena, 6–3 and 6–2. It was a demoralizing way to start. They were better than us in those two games, bottom line. And as it rained octopus, all that was going through our heads was, "We *have* to win our next game." Just two games in, it was already do or die.

We turned things around in our barn, though, fuelled by the wild fans in Toronto. In Game 2, Félix Potvin made some huge saves, and Dave Andreychuk finally got on the board, scoring two goals. We won 4–2. That momentum carried into Game 4. Once again, the fans were incredible. It was a physical game; tension was mounting. Ciccarelli was a pest in front of Potvin, getting in his face and jabbing at him all game. But he couldn't crack the Cat. We were tied 2–2 in the third when Andreychuk followed his wide shot behind the net and wrapped it around for the goal to put us up 3–2. Potvin shut down the Red Wings' assault after that, and as the seconds ticked down in the third period, the Gardens went wild.

I hadn't played well in our first two games. I scored two goals and an assist, but I wasn't myself. It's all about your mental state. But in Games 3 and 4, I'd picked up four assists and was plus three. I'd also managed to shut down Yzerman, who went scoreless. I was back. And we were back in the series, now tied two games apiece.

Now it was down to a best-of-three.

Back in Detroit for Game 5, the Red Wings flew out of the gates, taking a 4–1 lead. But we dug in and fought back to tie the game and force overtime. That's when Mike Foligno, one of our tough veteran leaders, took a pass in the slot from Wendel Clark and went five-hole on Tim Cheveldae to win it. It was huge. Foligno shook off his gloves and pirouetted in the air before we all embraced him. We'd won three in a row and were heading back to Toronto with a chance to finish the Red Wings off.

It didn't turn out the way we'd hoped. Instead of claiming victory in front of our fans, we fell apart. I checked Yzerman hard into the boards, and he needed five stitches to sew up the gash on his left cheek. We led 2–1 heading into the second, but that didn't last. The Red Wings tied it early in the second and then kept going. It was another rough battle. Yzerman hammered Peter Zezel into the boards, and he left with a concussion. We lost 7–3.

It came down to one last game to decide the series; and if we were going to move on, we'd have to do it back in Detroit. The pressure was on us now. Nikolai Borschevsky returned for Game 7 after breaking an orbital bone in Game 1. Burns switched up the lines, so I played alongside Clark and Borschevsky. That would be a key development.

We were battered and bruised after six vicious games. I had stitches below one eye and above the other. Burns had double-shifted me throughout the series. I was losing weight rapidly because of it, but I wasn't going to slow down.

Game 7 was an absolute classic. It was tense. It was wild. And it would come down to the end. We trailed 3–2 with just under three minutes to go in the third. The game went back and forth, back and forth, with chances at both ends. Then Clark took the puck into the corner on a rush and centred the puck. I was playing all over the place, and now I found myself alone in front of the net. The puck came to me, and as Cheveldae came out from his post, I quickly shot it, glove side. I didn't know where it went until I got around him. I was going glove side; that was all I knew. I just put my hands up in disbelief. It was my third point of the night. It just kind of brought us to life. *Maybe we can do this . . . Okay, here we go.*

Peter Zezel almost won it before the final buzzer on a wrap-around that Cheveldae managed to kick out right on the goal line. So we went to overtime, tied at three.

Sitting in the locker room before the extra period started, we didn't feel nervous. We were still alive, and that's all that mattered. It was almost like a mental shift. The pressure was on Detroit now.

Two and a half minutes into overtime, I made a move to come off the ice from a shift with Glenn Anderson and Andreychuk. Burns sent me right back out there to join Clark and Borschevsky. The play went into Detroit's end. I picked up the puck at the top of the left-hand faceoff circle and saw Bob Rouse streaking in on the other side. I slipped the puck across the ice to him, and he one-timed a shot that Borschevsky, who was standing just to the side of the crease, tipped into the Red Wings net. We ripped down the ice as the team poured off the bench. Our trainer, Brian Papineau, sprayed a water bottle up and down in celebration on the bench. Burns turned and saluted Cliff Fletcher, who was up in his box. It was the most emotional I'd seen our coach. It was emotional for all of us. It was the Leafs' first playoff series win since 1987. There was a photo of Borschevsky and me sitting side by side in the locker room after the celebration. He has this enormous grin on his face; he was so happy. We were moving on to the second round. It was magic.

We jumped on the bus, hauled our asses back across the border to Windsor and hopped on our short flight back to Toronto—for a little rest before starting round two.

Our first game against the St. Louis Blues was played just two days after our exhausting series with the Red Wings ended. The Blues had beaten the Chicago Blackhawks in four straight games, so they were well rested by the time we showed up. The first two games of the series were played at Maple Leaf Gardens, and neither offered a respite from the gruelling pace of playoff hockey. My former team had finished fourth in the division, and we hadn't lost to them in the regular season. They were technically the underdogs in the series, but they boasted offensive firepower courtesy of Craig Janney, Brett Hull and Brendan Shanahan. They also had Curtis Joseph in goal. When Cujo was playing, we were at a disadvantage. We experienced that first-hand in Game 1 at the Gardens.

The score was tied 1–1 through regulation, with Cujo stopping every attack. The game turned into a marathon. I was getting frustrated. We had so many chances, and Cujo was standing on his head. He was incredible. We knew he was a good goalie, but we didn't know quite how good. That overtime was just ridiculous. Joseph was clipped by Mike Foligno's skate with eight minutes left in the first overtime, and he had to leave the game to get his jaw stitched up. Guy Hebert tended the net for the next two and a half minutes. Even that didn't throw Joseph off.

The game went back and forth through the first overtime period and into the second. Finally, with just over three minutes to play in that second overtime frame, I picked up the puck behind the net and looked to make a pass. Blues defenceman Murray Baron was in front of the net, looking at me, with Borschevsky behind him in the high slot. Andreychuk was on the other side of the net, covered by Rick Zombo. I often set up back behind the net. I'd go back there and hide, and just lock in and try to make little saucer passes to anybody who was open. I learned to do that from Gretzky. But usually, I was passive. This time, I didn't know what I was doing back there. I have to admit that. I was just trying to buy time, going back and forth, waiting for Andy or Nicki to get open.

I could see them moving in front of the net. I went left, then curled back around and saw a little opening on Cujo, only a sliver. It was almost as though their defenceman had run into Cujo and he couldn't get over fast enough. I wrapped it around on my backhand. Four hours and 15 minutes after the drop of the puck—and after 64 shots on Joseph—it was over. I jumped into Todd Gill's arms and we hit the glass together. Everybody was jumping up and down. It was unreal. I don't know how many people really think they were at that game, but to this day I run into people all the time who tell me they were there. It became one of the most replayed goals in my career.

The second game was another battle of the goalies at the Gardens. Brett Hull and I both scored in the first period, knotting the game at one. After that, the show belonged to Potvin and Cujo. Once again, it took two overtime periods to determine a winner. Unfortunately, this time, Blues defenceman Jeff Brown swept in to score on a rebound off a shot from Craig Janney at 3:03 of the second overtime. This time, Joseph stopped 57 shots for the win, while Potvin kicked aside 38.

We got off to a great start in Game 3 in St. Louis, scoring the first two goals of the game, but we couldn't keep the Blues down, and they scored three straight to take the lead. We hammered away at Joseph in the dying seconds of the game, but once again, he kept the puck out and we lost it 4–3.

That put us behind in the series, two games to one. We knew that we had to win Game 4 to prevent the Blues from grabbing a stranglehold on the series. And we succeeded, coming out on top after another rough battle, winning 4–1 to take the series back to Toronto as a best-of-three.

Before Game 5, the finalists for the NHL's awards were released. The Maple Leafs hadn't had an individual award winner in 27 seasons, going all the way back to when Brit Selby won the Calder Trophy back in 1966. This time, it looked like we might have a chance. Félix Potvin was up for the Calder, as the league's best rookie. And Burns was up for another Jack Adams Award as the NHL's best coach. Meanwhile, I was a finalist for the Hart Trophy as the league's most valuable player, as well as the Selke Trophy, for the best defensive forward. The other finalists for the Selke were Dave Poulin of the Bruins and Joel Otto of Calgary. I was up against Pittsburgh's Mario Lemieux and Pat LaFontaine of Buffalo for the Hart. (It was the first time in Wayne Gretzky's career that he wasn't at least a finalist for the award; he missed half the season with a back injury.) I knew it was going to be tough being up against Mario for the Hart, but it was an incredible honour to be nominated. I felt I had a very good shot at the Selke, which was great—especially considering how much time I had dedicated in my career to playing hard at both ends of the ice.

We came out flying in Game 5, carrying over the momentum from our Game 4 win. We didn't miss a step. Cujo couldn't pull off his magic tricks this time. Dave Andreychuk scored two goals, and we went on to win 5–1 in front of our fans.

We were one game away from the conference final. But we were exhausted. We were playing every second day, with no real breaks. Burns wasn't letting us sit back and get soft. We held a full practice on our day off ahead of Game 6 back in St. Louis. We knew Cujo would bounce back, and we'd have to be in top form if we were going to avoid a seventh game.

Andreychuk opened the scoring with his 11th goal of the playoffs, which set a new Leafs record for playoff goals in a season. At the other end, Potvin held us in the game, stopping 25 shots. But in St. Louis, the Blues were incredibly hard to play against. It was a rough battle. And Cujo was just phenomenal. He made 40 stops to keep the Blues alive. We lost it 2–1—once again facing a Game 7 to decide our fate.

The thing about that series is that while we were outshooting them, with a guy like Cujo in net, it could have gone either way. We knew that.

We felt the heat heading into Game 7—literally. The Gardens was one of the hottest rinks to play in. We were dripping with sweat from the first shift of each game. And with Burns double-shifting me all series, I was shedding pounds like crazy. I was exhausted and bruised, but we just had to keep playing through it. After each game, I'd be on a table in the trainers' room, having an intravenous drip administered by our team doctor, getting electrolytes pumped right back into my system. Sometimes, after the treatment, it felt like I hadn't played at all.

Before the game, I had been standing in the hallway outside the Leafs' locker room, and I was approached by the *Toronto Star*'s Damien Cox. I was standing next to a row of portraits of Leafs greats: Syl Apps, Charlie Conacher, Turk Broda and Ted Kennedy. He asked me if I felt any pressure. Of course I did. I always felt pressure. But it was something that fuelled me on the ice. Off the ice, I tried to relax and joke around. I tried to keep from focusing on the pressure.

"Look, there's Mike Foligno," I joked, pointing to the photos of Maple Leaf legends.

"There's such a fine line between winning and losing," I told Cox, seriously now. "We can't be afraid of success."

What no one knew at the time was that I was battling the flu. I had skipped practice the day before as well as the morning skate ahead of Game 7. It actually worked out okay, because my preference was to just play the games anyway. I didn't like to practise—especially practices run by Pat "Line Up on the Boards" Burns.

It was the first Game 7 played at Maple Leaf Gardens since 1964, when Andy Bathgate scored the Stanley Cup winner. The fans were electric from the start, and that energy ignited us. Thankfully, this time the line between winning and losing was thick.

We were all over the Blues. We scored four goals in the first period. Then, in the second, Wendel Clark—who had already scored two of our goals—cut in over the blue line and knocked Joseph's mask off with a slapshot. It was a rocket, and it rattled him. Kent Manderville scored to give us five. And then I picked up a great pass from Dave Ellett just behind the Blues defence and scored on a semi-breakaway to make it six. The goal was my third point of the night and it gave me 22 in the playoffs, passing the team record of 21 that Darryl Sittler set in 1977.

The Gardens went crazy when the final buzzer sounded to close the book on our 6–0 win. It was a great, crazy feeling. The Gardens was surrounded by a sea of blue and white as fans spilled onto Carlton Street, continuing all the way down Yonge Street and beyond. They had waited so long—since 1978—for their team to make it this far into the playoffs. In part, we were feeling the energy that had been generated by the Jays' World Series win that fall. We hadn't even made the playoffs the year before, and now we had a chance to go to the Stanley Cup Final. It was crazy if you thought about it.

It was an incredible time to be in Toronto.

But there wouldn't be much time to savour the victory. We had just one day off before the first game of the Campbell Conference final against Wayne Gretzky and the Los Angeles Kings. So I was back in the chair, getting an IV—and then straight home to eat, rest up and prepare for L.A.

The Kings had knocked off Calgary and Vancouver, both teams that had finished ahead of them in the Smythe Division, to reach the conference final. I knew the Kings well from my days with the Flames. I thought we were a good match. (But one thing I never did was pick a team we'd rather play from another season; that would always come back to bite you.)

The Kings were a talented team. They had a couple of lines with firepower, and they had some workhorses. They were led by Gretzky, Luc Robitaille, Jari Kurri and Tony Granato. They had a lot of experience. On the blue line they had Paul Coffey—and Tim Watters, who was a little guy but played hard on you. They also had a 23-year-old named Rob Blake. He was lethal on power plays, especially when he was grouped with their elite scorers, so we knew we couldn't take too many penalties. But the Kings were also a tough team. In fact, they were one of the most penalized teams in the NHL, averaging more than 26 minutes a game in the box. In that department, they were led by Marty McSorley, who led the league with 399 penalty minutes during the regular season.

I knew what we were getting into right from the start. Before every game, I would read the game sheet and say, "Okay, this is the plan tonight: *this* guy is going to try to take my knee out, and *this* guy is going to try to take my head off." I knew who to watch out for. Certain guys would come up and talk to you, try to be your friend, and as soon as you had your head down, they were going to run you over. You knew who those guys were. You knew exactly what to look for against every opponent. When I saw McSorley's name, I knew to make sure I didn't cut through the middle.

The Kings came after me right from the start. That first tilt of the series wouldn't be remembered for the goals that were scored. It was a battle from start to finish. The most memorable action came in the third. I scored my second goal of the game and added two assists in the final frame. I also had a few big hits. I took out Alexei Zhitnik, who had his head down at the Kings blue line. He went down hard and stumbled back to the bench. Zhitnik came after me about seven minutes later with an elbow to the head as I passed the puck to Bill Berg, who put the game out of reach by giving us a three-goal lead with 4:39 to play. Then, with two and a half minutes left in the game, I cut across the blue line and dropped a pass to Anderson. I looked back to watch the pass. That was a big mistake. McSorley stepped in and hammered me. Thankfully, he missed my head with his elbow, but it felt like I'd hit a truck and I went down hard. It was a clean, fair hit on Marty's part. He caught me coming across the middle, watching my pass.

As I lay on the ice, trying to remember where I was, Clark went after McSorley. He always stood up for his teammates, and he wasn't going to let McSorley get a shot at me without paying a price. It was quite the battle. They went blow for blow as everyone else on the ice took a dance partner. McSorley came out of it with a pretty nice shiner.

When I got up, both sides were jawing at each other, and I went right to the Kings bench to let them know I wasn't going to stay down. I grabbed on to Darryl Sydor's stick and let my feelings be known. Things escalated from there. Fans got into it by shaking the glass and littering the ice with trash.

Before the end of the game, Burns and Kings coach Barry Melrose started shouting at each other across the benches—over top of me. Burns was making a point. He wanted Melrose to know there would be hell to pay. "Gretzky's next!" he shouted. Melrose snapped back with a comment. Had he managed to get through the crowd of security keeping him away from the Kings bench, I'm sure Burns would have taken Melrose out. If I could have put money on that fight, I'd have bet it all on Pat. He had so much emotion. He was the soul of our team. And just like Wendel, he'd fight for every single one of us.

After the game, I was a guest on *Hockey Night in Canada*, and my pal Don Cherry gave me a big kiss. He didn't shy away from picking sides. Cherry went after Melrose, calling him a "Billy Ray Cyprus" because his mullet looked like it belonged to country singer Billy Ray *Cyrus*, who'd had a big hit record the year before.

The tone was set for the rest of the series. Burns said he had lost all respect for the Kings, noting that if Ken Baumgartner, our enforcer, had been in the lineup and done the same thing to Gretzky that McSorley had done to me, there would have been hell to pay.

I'd always remembered Brian Sutter's advice to me back when I was with the Blues, warning me not to wake up our opponents' most aggressive guys. Well, now I considered myself to be the target. And going into certain games, I felt like *they* should have said, "Don't wake him up" about me. Maybe they should have just let me sleep some nights. That's how I thought about it. Because as soon as I got hit—as soon as someone gave me a cheap shot—I was thinking, "Okay . . . Game on." It made me compete that much harder.

I took practice off the next day to get some rest, which aroused suspicion among reporters that I was injured. It was just a routine I got into to survive those playoffs, while playing up to 40 minutes a night. I'd sneak in and get some treatment from the trainers and sneak out before the media saw me. It was the only time I really had to recover between games. Burns was great. He'd distract the reporters and put any rumours to rest. "Dougie had to go back to his planet and rest," he said.

In Game 2, I scored on the power play early, and we led 2–1 four minutes into the first. It felt like we were playing in a packed sauna, the Gardens was so muggy. Before the end of the first period, McSorley and I exchanged words and were pushing each other. I gave him a very purposeful headbutt, which I later claimed happened because I slipped. We both went to the box for roughing, so I got away with one there. I didn't knock his teeth out or anything, but I shouldn't have done it.

The Kings shut us down the rest of the game and came back to win 3–2—sending us to Los Angeles with the series tied at one game each. At the L.A. Forum, we got exactly the kind of reception we expected. Fans brought doughnuts to throw at Burns. It was getting ugly. The fans also had special signs made up for me, which they flashed during the Canadian national anthem. One side of the signs said "Head Butt Gilmour," and when they flipped them around they said "Butt Head Gilmour." Clever.

I didn't pay attention to it, though. The Kings' fans booed every time I touched the puck. They had a lot of words to say to me every game. To me, that always meant I was doing something right.

We split Games 3 and 4 in Los Angeles, with 4–2 decisions for both teams. Their building was just as electric as ours. They also had some big-time Hollywood support. Actors like John Candy, Sylvester Stallone, Mary Hart and James Woods were at the games. Hockey's popularity was building in California, and it was all because of Gretzky. The trade that brought him to the Kings put the franchise on the map.

Thankfully, Gretzky was relatively quiet in both of those games, just as he'd been all series. He didn't score his first goal of the series until Game 4. While we could have taken comfort in knowing the greatest hockey player ever wasn't playing his best, we knew better. It was only a matter of time before Gretzky started playing like Gretzky again—and we had to finish the Kings off before he got there.

For the third straight series, we were knotted at two games each after four. It was another long haul across the continent, back to Toronto for Game 5. We chartered the flights, so guys were able to lie down across entire rows and get some much-needed rest while we were in the air. The trainers would fuel us up with some good food and get us hydrated. It was like a physical recovery centre in the sky.

We battled back from a 2–0 deficit in Game 5 to send the game to overtime, even though the Kings dominated us most of the game. Potvin had to make 41 saves in the game. Then, with just 39 seconds left in the first sudden-death period, Glenn Anderson batted his own rebound between Kelly Hrudey's legs to give us the win. "We pulled a rabbit out of the hat tonight," Burns said after the game. "We weren't very good." But still, Leafs fans would take it—and so would we.

Toronto was one win away from going to the Stanley Cup Final for the first time since 1967.

With a chance to finish off the Kings in L.A. in Game 6, our captain dominated the game. We put ourselves in a hole with a few bad penalties and trailed 4–2 with just nine minutes to go in the third period. Clark, who already had one of our goals, added two more to almost single-handedly keep us alive. With just over a minute to go in the game, Clark came on the ice as the extra attacker with Potvin on the bench. I saw him cutting in and passed it to him at the top of the circle and ducked behind the net as he took two strides and loaded up his signature wrist shot. I knew if it missed the net and hit me, I'd be dead. Instead, it went top shelf on Hrudey's glove side. We all threw our hands up. It was an incredible comeback—and we were about to head to overtime, one goal away from the Cup final.

Early in overtime, Anderson was called for boarding, putting the Kings on the power play. I was up against Gretzky on the faceoff on the next play. We both went for the puck after Jamie Macoun blocked his shot. Gretzky missed my stick while trying to take the puck and came up underneath. His stick hit me in the face and cut me. Kerry Fraser, the referee, wasn't in position to see it. At the time, the rule was that if the referee didn't see a high stick, the linesmen could call it, but it would be five minutes and a game misconduct. If Fraser called it, it would have been just a two-minute penalty. We were at the Forum in Los Angeles. If a linesman called a penalty that would toss Gretzky out of the game, there was going to be a riot in that arena. In my mind, if Fraser didn't see the high stick and his linesmen did, they could have agreed to say that Fraser had seen it and given Gretzky a two-minute penalty. Then it would have been four on four. That would have solved everything.

Instead, there was no call. I was in the locker room getting eight stitches in my chin when I heard the roar less than a minute later. The game was over; we had lost. When I found out it was Gretzky who directed a pass into the net, I felt a little sick—I knew the beast was waking up. This was going to be trouble.

I was livid at the time. We all were. But to be honest, I got over it pretty quickly. It's something that happened; it was frustrating and disappointing. I was never mad at Gretzky. The incident happened quickly, and it was a complete accident. And I wouldn't want Kerry Fraser's job. He was in a no-win situation there. There was only one referee at the time, too. If one of the linesmen had seen it, he could have called it. That was my only issue with how it went down. But I have no real animosity about it. I've seen Kerry many times since then, and we're friends. But whenever someone asks me about Fraser (and they often do), I tell them that I have only one small regret: I wish I would have played one more game while he was reffing, and I would have skated right up to him and messed up his hair. Then I would have just skated off the ice: "See you, guys. I'm done!"

Once again, for the third time in the 1993 playoffs, we would play one last game to decide whether our season was over or we'd go on. This time, a trip to the Stanley Cup Final was on the line. To go from having missed the playoffs to being on the cusp of the final in just one year—we had a lot to be proud of at that point. Going into the season, if someone had told me we had a chance to play Game 7 of the conference final at home? Yeah, I'd be all in. Obviously, there was a lot of bitterness because of the non-call when we got home, but as a team we just needed to focus and put it all in perspective. We tried to stay in our own little world as a team, together.

We were warriors on the ice. I did some things that I normally didn't do on the ice. I was vicious. We all were. There were times when I took my helmet off and thought, "Did I really do that?" I mean, I actually headbutted McSorley. I knew that wasn't right. But we were willing to do anything to win. We felt like a team that was destined to win. It was an incredible feeling. Burns captured our mentality best when he told us, "Just bleed, boys." We did. And we would have kept on bleeding. Back in Toronto for Game 7, we were ready to bleed out on that ice.

But unfortunately, our sense of destiny ran up against the greatest player the game has ever known. As I mentioned, Gretzky was good in the series, but he wasn't his usual *great* self. At that point, Gretzky had three fewer points than I had in the playoffs. He was his typical humble self after forcing Game 7, pointing out that he wasn't superhuman and that he wasn't going to score four points a night—but when he did do something, it had to be "big." He wasn't kidding.

Ahead of Game 7, one of the local Toronto reporters wrote an article pointing out just how average Gretzky had been. Well, talk about waking up the beast. You don't tell the best player that he's average going into Game 7 of a conference final. He'd just scored the overtime winner, and we all knew there was more where that came from. You'd better believe Gretzky read the article. If I had been his coach, I'd have posted it in the dressing room. If somebody has to say something about your team or your player, you post that up. You want it to be shown. You want to piss off the target of the comments.

In Game 7 at home, Wayne Gretzky showed us why he is the greatest hockey player of all time. We fought hard, and we were chasing them all the way, but they were on a roll. The Kings were leading 4–3 late in the third period when Gretzky completed a hat trick by banking the puck off Dave Ellett's skate from behind the net, and it went over Potvin's pad. It could have been demoralizing. But moments later, Ellett got it back, scoring to make it 5–4 with two minutes left in the game. Burns pulled Potvin for the extra man, and we fought and fought frantically to get the tying goal. We had a couple of good chances with about 15 seconds to go, but it didn't happen. It just wasn't destined to be the way we'd thought. We ran out of time.

When the final buzzer went, the Kings poured onto the ice. Gretzky had put up three goals and an assist right when the Kings needed him the most. They were moving on to face the Montreal Canadiens for the Stanley Cup. We were going home. Clark smashed his stick, breaking it. But then we shook the Kings' hands and wished them well. It had been an all-out war. There was dignity in losing. We had played 21 games in 41 nights. And we left everything we had on the ice.

In the end, the best player in the world beat us. It was as simple as that.

15

BENCHED

LOSING TO WAYNE GRETZKY and the Kings didn't sit well with me, so I was already working out for the next season by the time, just a few weeks after we'd been eliminated, that I was awarded the Selke Trophy as the NHL's best defensive forward. I finished second in voting for the Hart Trophy, which went to Mario Lemieux, who had missed a month of the season to be treated for Hodgkin's disease and still came back to score 160 points in 60 games. But the Selke was an incredible honour, and I was thrilled to receive it.

I knew it was going to be hard to top the season I'd just had. Scoring 127 points wasn't easy. But I was excited about what we'd accomplished as a team and where we were heading.

I felt as good as I had in years. I'd managed to spend some downtime with my parents back at their house on Loughborough Lake. I was no longer pale and sickly looking. My bruises were starting to heal. I even had a new haircut, cut short on the sides and hairsprayed straight up like I'd been electrocuted. I swear it was stylish at the time. My 30th birthday was just around the corner, and I felt as good as I had when I was 24.

But there was another reason why I was feeling so good.

At the time, there were some big changes going on in my life. My first marriage had ended before the start of the 1992–93 season. So that year I'd been newly single. I dated a bit here and there—until I met Amy Cable.

I first met Amy after the team had the intrasquad Blue and White Game in training camp in the fall of 1992, at a rink in northwest Toronto. Wendel's team beat mine—and I was pissed off about how I'd played. When it was over, I drove back to the Gardens and hopped on the bike for an hour and did a full workout. By the time I got out of the shower and dressed, a concert was starting in the rink, by a guy named Morrissey. I'd never heard of him. I sat there for about 10 minutes. (It wasn't my kind of music.) But that's when I ran into Amy, who was working as an usherette. She was stunning—an actual model, I'd later discover. And she was smart and funny. But she was dating someone else.

Not long after that, I started seeing her at P.M. Toronto with her friends after our games. They'd come and hang out with us at the back of bar. We became friends, but nothing more than that. Around that time, my daughter's favourite song was "Achy Breaky Heart," so I took her to the Billy Ray Cyrus concert at the Gardens. Amy was working near where we were standing for the concert. She showed us to some better seats that no one was using.

Soon after that, I saw her at the bar and asked how she was doing. She said she wasn't doing great; she had just broken up with her boyfriend. Suddenly, *I* was doing great. We started talking on the phone and hanging out more after my games. I gave her and her friend a key to my apartment so they could change out of their work clothes before coming to the bar with us.

But nothing happened between us until after Game 7 against Detroit in the 1993 playoffs. Amy was watching the game at the bar with her friends. The team flew back to Toronto right after the game. I didn't get home until one o'clock in the morning. When I walked in the door, Amy was there, waiting to surprise me.

We were together all through those playoffs. That's really when our relationship began. And it moved quickly. The first time I took Amy anywhere in public, as a couple, was a few days after we lost to the Kings. Steve Stavro had a party at his massive place—it was like a big ranch—outside of the city. The party started at 4 p.m. Everyone who worked with the team was there—players, coaching staff, trainers, doctors and everyone else. We had a nice dinner and drinks in this party area out back. And then, around 9 p.m., the lights started flashing on and off—giving us the "party's over" signal. Evidently, Stavro wasn't one for late nights.

Soon, Amy and I decided to move in together. My place next to the Gardens was terrible. It was small and cramped—and the furniture wasn't even mine! So I bought a new warehouse condo in Toronto's west end, just off of Bloor Street a few blocks from Christie Pits Park. Almost every day through the summer of '93, I'd run down Dufferin Street to Christie Pits, where I'd charge up the steep incline behind the backstop of the baseball diamond. That summer, people must have wondered what the guy in a ball cap and bicycle shades was doing running up and down—and up and down—the hill in the park, but the disguise must have worked, because no one seemed to recognize me.

The hill was perfect for off-season training, but I must have looked ridiculous. I'd sprint up the hill as fast as I could, hustle back down, and sprint back up. I tried to do as many lengths as I could in 15 minutes, and then I'd try to do the same number in 14 and a half, and so on. "What's that guy doing over there?" people must have thought, watching me go back and forth like that for 30 minutes. "He's not getting anything accomplished!" It was exhausting, but nothing compared to the gruelling endurance test that the 1993 playoffs had been. We'd just been so close to the Stanley Cup Final. I was determined to do anything in my power to help get us another opportunity. So I ran, and I ran, and

I ran—knowing that every extra sprint would help us get there, somehow.

That summer, I bought a brand new Harley-Davidson Fat Boy. I'd picked it up on the counsel of Pat Burns, who was a big Harley guy. That summer, the players on the team had done a promotional photo called "Pat's Garage." We all sat around in front of an old auto body shop, looking like we worked there. I'm sitting on my Harley in the photo. I loved that bike. But I wouldn't get to drive it for long.

When training camp started on September 12, I rolled up to Maple Leaf Gardens on it. I drove up through the garage door at the Gardens—just off Wood Street, where the Zamboni would come out—and parked at the bottom of the ramp, near the entrance where the visiting team would walk down to their dressing room. Just as I shut off the engine and was pulling off my helmet, Cliff Fletcher walked in.

"When you have a chance, come on up and see me," he said.

Cliff's office was up on the second floor, with all the other management. Usually, if you were going up there, you were going up there *for a purpose.* So I went up to see Cliff like a kid who'd been sent to the principal's office. When I walked in the door, he got right to the point.

"*What* are you doing?" he said.

"What do you mean?" I asked.

"A Harley?" he said. "Where do you want to start? What if you fall? What if you get hurt?"

I just stood there like a middle-schooler taking a scolding.

"You'll have to explain to me, explain to your peers, to your coaches—and the fans," Cliff continued. "That includes the media. Have you ever looked at your contract? You know you're not supposed to be riding."

I didn't get a word in.

"If you want to ride in the off-season and I'm not around, fine—I know a lot of guys do it," he said. "But to training camp!"

"Okay," I said. "I got it."

Fully chastised, I drove the Harley home after practice for the first and last time. When I saw Pat the next day, I told him the bad news.

"Burnsie, I gotta sell this," I said. I'd only had the bike for about two months, tops!

Being the Harley connoisseur he was, Pat knew a guy.

Fletcher could be intimidating in his own way, but he was a class act. I loved playing for organizations that he was in charge of. At the start of the 1993–94 season, I signed a brand new five-year deal with Toronto. Salaries around the league had been rising, and Fletcher felt the $1.2 million I was earning was low. He wanted to lock me in for the long term. The deal was worth $3 million (Canadian) a year. That was a big deal at the time, but it turned out to be modest because by the end of my contract, guys were making almost twice as much as I was. With the new contract, I arranged to have $1 million deferred, so each year I'd be making $2 million—and after taxes, it was $1 million. The contract worked well for me because I was going to be 34 years old when it ended and I'd be in a position to retire. At the time, that was a real consideration for me. The deal was easy to agree to. I was in the prime of my career and exactly where I wanted to be. I'd have been happy to have ended my career as a Leaf.

The deal was finalized during our first stretch of games that season, when it seemed like we were unbeatable. It was another incredible time for sports in Toronto. As the streak went on, the Toronto Blue Jays made it to the World Series for the second straight year. Once again, the city was full of excitement.

We didn't think much of the streak at first, but the media were already making a big deal of it when we won our first three games of the season . . . then four . . . then five. Burns did his best to keep us in line. We made it six in a row with a 6–3 win in Detroit. And then seven straight by beating the Hartford Whalers 7–2.

Burns wasn't having any of it. He rolled his eyes when people started talking about us having a chance to break the Oilers' 15-game undefeated streak to start the 1984–85 campaign. "So, we're allowed a tie now, are we?" he joked, when reporters asked him about it. "I'd hoped all this talk about streaks was over."

The Jays played Game 6 of the World Series against the Philadelphia Phillies at the SkyDome on Saturday, October 23. The same night, we were in Tampa Bay, playing against the Lightning, with a chance to win our ninth in a row, which would set the new record for consecutive wins to start a season. Because of Joe Carter and his ninth-inning home run, not too many people will remember that we won 2–0.

In the third period of that game, I took issue with Roman Hamrlik, who grabbed my head from behind and twisted it back. I spun around and returned the favour with a half a dozen punches. Seemed like a fair exchange at the time. But the league felt differently. I was called in for a disciplinary hearing before we played Chicago in our next game, a few days later. At first, it looked like I was going to miss the game against the Blackhawks, but thankfully I made it into the lineup and was later given just a $500 fine. (I thought the whole process was ridiculous.) We went on to beat the Blackhawks 4–2 to win our 10th straight game. Potvin made 42 saves in the game. He was a huge part of our early success.

Our record-setting start just added to the energy in the city, as Toronto revelled in back-to-back World Series wins. It was exciting, but we tried not to get ahead of ourselves. It was a long season, after all. And when the Montreal Canadiens beat us 5–2 at the Forum to end the streak a couple of days later, Burns was relieved.

"I'm glad it's over," he told reporters after the loss.

But as much as he seemed to resent the distraction of the winning streak, I really think we owed that historic run to Burns. By no means should we have won all those games.

But Burns helped us find ways to do things we should not have been able to do. We weren't the most talented team in the league. We had a great goalie in Potvin, who stole some games for us. And my line got off to a strong start, which helped put some pucks in the net. But Burns was the main guy who brought it all together. That's what he did so well. He drove us to accomplish things we otherwise shouldn't have been able to do.

That's not to say that he and I always saw eye to eye. Burns was particular about a lot of things in the game. But there was one rule that pissed him off more than most if you broke it: "Do not lose the puck at the opposition blue line." Especially in the first two minutes of the game or the last two minutes of a period. It didn't matter who you were. You could have been Gretzky, for all Burns cared. If you gave up the puck at the blue line, he was going to let you have it.

Partway through the season, I tried to get a little too creative carrying the puck on the first shift of a game at the Gardens, and I got stripped. The other team went down and scored on the giveaway. When I got to the bench, Burns didn't say a word to me. Andreychuk and I sat next to each other as Burns cycled out the other lines and didn't put us on. After a few shifts, we still weren't moving.

"Are you kidding me?" I said to Andreychuk.

He shook his head.

"You make that play every game," he said. "Don't worry about it."

But more and more time went by, and we just sat there. I looked back at Burns, but he didn't acknowledge me.

Five minutes went by. Then 10. I was so angry.

"Don't worry about it," Andreychuk said.

Andy was always like that. He never got emotional, on or off the ice. He'd get slashed and hacked in front of the net and just stand there taking it because they couldn't move him. He was being benched because of something I'd done, but he didn't get upset about it.

"We'll get back out," he said. "Watch."

"No," I said. "I'm pissed."

Finally, with a minute to go in the first period, Burns sent us back out. The fans cheered when we got on the ice. Everyone in the Gardens knew I'd been benched. That just pissed me off even more. Usually, when I was on Burns's bad side, I'd just take it. But this time I was livid. I was fine missing a shift or two, but being benched for the whole period? I didn't know if he was going to keep benching me for the rest of the game.

In my mind, I wasn't thinking about the mistake I made; I was thinking about scoring a goal so it wouldn't matter. That's how you fix it. But Burns wouldn't even let me play!

Between periods, I stormed into Burns's office. I looked at Mike Murphy and Mike Kitchen, our assistant coaches, and said, "Excuse me"—which more or less meant "Get the hell out." They did.

"Are you kidding me?" I shouted at Burns. "Why would you do that?"

Burns just looked at me calmly.

"Doug, sit down," he said.

I didn't sit. I was pissed. I wanted answers.

"Why would you embarrass me like that?" I said.

Burns kept it simple.

"Fuckin' relax," he said. "What did you do on your first shift?"

"Okay, I lost the puck," I said. "They scored."

"So, if another guy on our team does it, I've got to bench him," he said, "but I can't bench you? A rule is a rule."

He had me there. I was a leader on the team, and that meant I shouldn't expect to be treated differently than any other player. In his mind, it was important that he treat everyone the same. It didn't matter that I'd been a finalist for the Hart Trophy a season earlier. I might as well have been just another rookie. He had to show the other guys. There was a higher chance that I was going to make a mistake at the blue line because I'd be carrying the puck in, trying to do something creative. But the other guys were going to dump it in. Still, that didn't exempt me from the rules. They were *his* rules and we had to follow them.

Burns was right.

And at the same time, he wasn't annoyed that I was challenging him. He didn't shout or get angry. He just calmly explained his reasoning. It wasn't about me; it was about the team. At the same time, I showed him that it affected me. I showed him that I wanted to play. And in his eyes, that was just as important. He *wanted* me to be mad.

"Okay, okay," I said, walking out. "I got it."

I made the mistake. I'm the one who did it, and I had to deal with the consequences—along with linemates, who were benched with me. I couldn't help but think that if I had made that play and we'd scored, none of this would've happened. I didn't make that point to Burns. I just wanted an answer and I got it. And I respected it.

Burnsie's position was you should look in the mirror and not lie to yourself. Afterwards, when media asked about why he benched me, he just said, "Why don't you go ask him?" We were accountable for the way we played. If I didn't play well, I was going to have to own it. If anyone else had made a mistake that cost us a goal, they'd have to own it, too.

And again, he had his whipping boys—his words. You know, your fourth line and your fifth line, the guys who weren't playing. Young guys. He'd skate them and be harder on them.

But he earned our respect. It was clear that he was for real. He was serious about his game plan. You're going to live and die by it, so don't screw it up.

He wasn't just thinking about the game we were playing. He was thinking about the bigger picture. It was his way of preparing us for the next game.

Burns knew when to relax and when to lay into us. There were times when he'd fork over several hundred bucks and tell us to go out as a group and have a night out on him. He knew the importance of that. And then there were times when Burns definitely wasn't about being your pal. He knew how to motivate certain guys. You need to ride the guys differently; nobody's the same. He knew when, sometimes, guys needed to hear, "Good job. Keep going."

I look back now and I can almost understand it better. Burns was hard and he was demanding, but he was respectful. He wanted us to be a *team*: to win and lose as a team, to go out as a team, to have fun as a team. We had incredible camaraderie. We hung out together a lot. One time, Potvin asked me to go with him to some concert at a venue called the Opera House. I had no idea what I was getting into. No one really knew this, but Potvin was really into punk music. So, he took me to this punk concert. I stood at the back of the place, sipping a beer, and wasn't sure where Potvin was. Then I looked up and saw him jumping around the mosh pit. It was crazy. Our goalie looked like he was in the middle of a massive rumble. I went in and grabbed him out of there. I couldn't let our goalie get crushed in a mosh pit! If I couldn't ride a motorcycle, he shouldn't have been allowed to go to punk concerts.

That season, there was a "Leaf for a Day" charity event where a fan would pay for a chance to come skate in a practice with us. This guy paid about $10,000 to charity. Burns treated him like he was just another player, making him stretch with us and skate with us—everything we did, he did.

To start practice, we did these sprints from blue line to blue line for about five minutes. This poor guy was gassed. Afterwards, we sat and stretched in the centre-ice circle, and he was huffing and puffing the whole time, trying to catch his breath. Well, because he was supposed to be part of the team, we treated him like we'd treat another rookie. Before he went on the ice, I took his wood sticks and made a small cut with a saw just above the blade. The spot was covered by a sticker, so I peeled it off and replaced it so he couldn't see that the sticks had been doctored. After we stretched, Burns called for a shooting drill. I passed a puck to our Leaf for a Day, and his blade flew off. We all started laughing, but he had no clue. He was just like "Oh my God, these guys pass hard!" He grabbed his other stick from the bench. Another pass, and his stick shattered again. We were howling, but he didn't catch on. The poor guy paid a fortune to be there, so of course we gave him a couple new sticks to use, for his trouble. Fortunately, he didn't grab the water bottle whose cap I had loosened, or he'd have dumped water all over himself, too. (I would have died laughing, but that probably would have been a bit too much.)

The fans in Toronto were great. At the time, it seemed like everyone in the city was a Leafs fan. We went out as a team a lot, and for the most part it was fine—but we had to pick our spots. Usually, fans were just excited and incredibly kind. Unfortunately, a few times, things went a bit too far. Once, I was asked to pick the SUNshine Girl for the *Toronto Sun*. I didn't really want to do it, so I just told them to make a selection for me. A couple days later, one of the Leafs' longstanding employees, Jeannie Ferreira, called down to the locker room and said that I had a visitor. I went up to the lobby to see who it was. It was the woman I had "selected" to be the SUNshine Girl.

"Hi, Doug," she said. "It's kind of fate that we met like this . . ."

Uh-oh.

I told her I was in a happy, committed relationship and that picking her as the SUNshine Girl was *not* an indication that I wanted to date her.

When we moved to a larger home in the Fallingbrook area in the Beaches, it didn't get much better. Once again, word quickly spread that we were living there. People knocked on my door every day. Some would stop by to take a photo or just get a glimpse of the place. Sometimes fan mail would show up. A few parents came up to the door and asked if I'd be able to attend their kid's birthday. Sometimes, it was fine. Other times, it was a bit much. But I really enjoyed the neighbourhood. People would stop and say hi. They were genuinely pleasant and friendly. I could walk down the street to Queen Street and grab a bite at the Sunset Grill. It was a cool spot. I always loved living in neighbourhoods like that. It reminded me of Kingston.

But for a time in that 1993–94 season, it got scary. Usually, any mail that came in for us was sorted upstairs in the offices, where an employee would help sort it and arrange for us to sign cards to send back to the fans. But one day, early in the season, a letter was dropped off to Jeannie in the office in the lobby of the Gardens. There were always people coming and going, so no one was sure who had brought it in.

It was odd, but at first I didn't take it seriously. I actually thought someone was pulling a prank on me. But then, every couple of weeks, another letter would arrive. They were angry in nature, and they basically accused me of ignoring the sender, who was anonymous. I kept them in my stall and tried not to worry about it. I looked around the room suspiciously to see which guys were snickering. At first, I went to Fletcher and told him I thought someone was pranking me, but that I wanted to let him know, just in case. Then I tried to forget about it.

But then a woman called my brother, Dave, at the bar we had opened up in Kingston, called Gilmour's, saying that I wasn't giving her the time of day and that she was going to kill me. She called more than a dozen times over the course of a few days. She spoke in a low whisper every time. The calls were traced to a public phone booth in downtown Toronto.

The final letter that arrived was the one that really got to me. It said that on a specific day, I was going to die.

With that, I finally told Burns about the letters. Harking back to his days as a cop, he took matters into his own hands. He informed the Toronto police and got them involved. The police took the letters and found fingerprints, but they didn't match anyone with a record. A few days before the date I was told I'd die, there were five cop cars waiting for me outside the Gardens after practice. They escorted me home. There was a marked car in front of and behind the house, and then several other unmarked cop cars surrounding us. They were stationed outside of our home and would escort us everywhere we went.

On game day, they were stationed all around the Gardens. We parked across the street behind the rink, so there were cop cars lined up there as well. During the game, there were more cops posted around our bench than usual. Afterwards, the officers would scan the mob of people looking to get autographs to make sure there was no one suspicious in line. I never found out who it was. But as soon as the police got involved, the letters stopped coming and I never heard from her again—so I can only assume she was close enough to realize that the cops were on the lookout. It only lasted for a few weeks, in total, and I tried to keep it out of my mind. It might have been a legitimate threat, or maybe just someone who didn't like me, or even just a bad joke. But when my life was threatened, I have to admit, it got to me.

16

'94

We finished the 1993–94 regular season in second place in the new Central Division, with 98 points, just behind the Detroit Red Wings. For the third time in my career, I scored more than 100 points—27 goals and 84 assists, for 111 points, which ranked fourth in the NHL. My linemate Andreychuk scored 53 goals and finished with 99 points, which tied his career best. Meanwhile, Clark had one of his best seasons, scoring 46 goals despite playing only 64 games because of injuries.

But after our hot start to the season, we did cool off a bit—something Burns had warned us about—going 11–14–7 over our next 32 games. We were holding on to first place in the division at the trade deadline when Cliff Fletcher shipped

Glenn Anderson to the New York Rangers for another soon-to-be Hall of Famer, Mike Gartner, but we had a rough final month of the season and looked to be in a downward spiral heading into the playoffs. But once the post-season began, we were eager to do some damage again.

We faced the Chicago Blackhawks in the first round. We won the first two games at home at the Gardens but lost the next two in Chicago. Late in Game 5, back at the Gardens, I twisted my right ankle in a small battle on the boards with Gary Suter. Afterwards, I took one more faceoff in our end, but I went right to the bench as the play went up the ice. It felt like I had snapped a bone in my ankle. Thankfully, Mike Eastwood jumped on the ice for me and ended up scoring the only goal of the game. But I couldn't return to the ice after that. I went for X-rays right after the game. They came back negative, but it was a severe sprain and my ankle was swollen like a grapefruit. The injured ligament also caused sharp pain in my calf.

With Game 6 in Chicago's barn, the media were wondering if I'd sit out in case the Blackhawks managed to force a seventh game. I skated that morning and could barely put any weight on my ankle. It looked like I *was* going to have to sit the game out. But there was no way I was about to let that happen.

"Well, I realize there's that seventh game and what it might mean," I said. "But it's not my style to sit out when there's a way I can play."

Before the warm-up in Game 6, I had our team doctor inject my right ankle with novocaine. He put four needles in—two in the front of my ankle, two in the back. I *hated* needles. When I was a kid, I used to get them all the time to treat hay fever. They still freaked me out as an adult. That was actually the worst part of it! But if the novocaine could take away the pain for a bit, I figured my ankle could heal later.

In fact, it felt like the novocaine took my whole foot away. I couldn't feel a thing. When I first stepped on the ice, I started to wobble. I looked down and realized my skate wasn't tight enough. I didn't know how tight to tie it, because I couldn't feel my foot! During the game, I had no control. If I went to kick the puck, I wouldn't know if I was hitting it or just striking the ice. In the end, I only played about 10 minutes the whole game. Burns would put me out for power plays and a few regular shifts, but I didn't really do anything else. Thankfully, we eliminated the Blackhawks with another close 1–0 win. It was the last hockey game that would be played at the old Chicago Stadium, with the brand new United Center slated to open the following season.

As soon as we got on the plane, the trainers put my foot in a special inflatable cast to make sure my ankle wouldn't swell with the change in cabin pressure. Back in Toronto, our doctors put me through a quick round of rehab, with ultrasound treatments and a series of exercises.

Our second-round opponents were the San Jose Sharks. Even though the Sharks were only in their third season in the NHL and had finished third in the Pacific Division with a sub-.500 record, they were still going to be a tough test for us.

Their lineup, which featured Sergei Makarov, Igor Larionov, Todd Elik, Sandis Ozolinsh and Jamie Baker, had a lot of skill. We'd had a hard time with them all season—they'd battled us to a pair of 2–2 ties and beaten us 2–1 and 5–3 in our four meetings—and this series wasn't going to be any different. They took us right to the limit. We split the first two games in Toronto, and then they beat us 5–2 back in their Shark Tank.

Several of the members of the band Metallica were at all the games. They were big hockey fans. After the game, about 10 of us went to a bar across from our hotel called San Jose Live to have a couple of beers. Singer James Hetfield and drummer Lars Ulrich were both there. The bar had those little arcade-style basketball hoops with a timer, so we played against them. We were only there for about 40 minutes, but it was so cool—playing basketball against Metallica! Even though they were Sharks fans, they were also huge hockey fans. They wished us luck—but, of course, they hoped we'd lose.

We had a day off before Game 4. My day was simple: rest, food, rehab, repeat. We needed every extra day we had. The doctors had me on a strict regime.

It seemed to work. We came back hard in Game 4, knowing how hard it would be to stay in the series if the Sharks picked up three wins. We took that game 8–3. It was a good outing for me. I managed to tie the franchise record of five points in a playoff game, scoring a goal and adding four assists. Before each game, I was still getting a couple of injections of novocaine to numb the pain in my ankle and calf.

The Sharks refused to back down. They won Game 5 at home—this was a 2–3–2 series, which meant we had to play three in a row out west. Then, back in Toronto, they pushed us to overtime and the brink of elimination in Game 6. Clark scored a pair of goals in regulation, and we went to overtime knotted at two.

We got lucky early on, when a Sharks shot hit the crossbar. We didn't even have a shot on net until 8:43 into the period. Thankfully, it went in. I had carried the puck behind the net, and it managed to find its way out to Mike Gartner, who put it past Arturs Irbe. The Gardens erupted in relief. We were alive, but only by the skin of our teeth.

Just before Game 7, I came down with a sinus infection. "Great!" I thought. "I can barely walk, and now I can barely breathe."

When I woke up that morning, I called Burns.

"Can't come to the rink this morning," I said. "My sinus."

"Oh, another thing," he said. "What else is going to happen?"

I skipped the morning skate, but it would take a lot more than a sinus infection and a busted leg to keep me out of a Game 7. Before the game, I learned of a remarkable home remedy for sinus relief. Our trainer slathered my nose and cheekbones with one of those muscle-relief balms, the kind that heats up. About a minute later, everything stuffing up my nose came rushing out. It was disgusting—but effective.

I still wasn't 100 per cent, but it didn't matter so much because, once again, Wendel Clark and Félix Potvin were the heroes. Our captain scored two goals in the first two periods to give us a nice lead heading into the third. San Jose had a 26–11 advantage in shots by the end of the second, but Potvin kicked aside everything the Sharks threw at him. Mark Osborne and I both managed to get pucks past Irbe in the third, matching the pair the Sharks finally scored on the Cat. We won it 4–2.

And for the second season in a row, we were advancing to the conference final after squeaking through a seven-game series. Once again, we were battered, but we'd been here before.

Whenever I was able to spend some time at home during those playoffs, I'd just pass out on the couch. I must have looked like a complete mess: I didn't have my front teeth in, my eyes were black, my face was cut up, and I had this balloon cast inflated around my leg to keep all the swelling down. My ankle had healed for the most part, and I wasn't taking any more shots of novocaine, but there were still plenty of tender spots.

We had to keep all the blinds and curtains closed. We were still on edge because of the threats I'd received. Every time the doorbell rang, we answered it cautiously. My sister Donna was staying with us at the time while she was going to hairdressing school. She was there through everything that winter. One day as she got off the streetcar, a man started following her. He caught up to her and asked if she knew whether Doug Gilmour lived on the street she was turning onto. She just said she had no clue and kept walking, but it freaked her out. During the San Jose series that spring, several pieces of women's underwear were left on the lawn and draped in the bushes. Donna and Amy collected them all with one of my sticks. It was insane!

Partially rested and more or less healed, I felt good heading into our series against Vancouver. The Canucks had been off for several days after beating the Dallas Stars in five games to advance.

Once again, we'd play two at home before playing the next three games of the series on the road. That format really pissed Burns off.

The Canucks had a very good team. They were led by Pavel Bure, a 60-goal scorer that season, as well as guys like Geoff Courtnall, Cliff Ronning and Trevor Linden. Vancouver also had a pretty good goalie in Kirk McLean. We knew it was going to be a tough series.

We managed to take the first game in overtime but dropped the second game at home 4–3. Burns had warned us that we needed to take both games at home if we wanted to counter the advantage the Canucks would have with three straight games in the Pacific Coliseum.

The problem was that we were out of gas. We'd never have admitted it at the time, but we were exhausted. Burns tried to rally us, and we fought as hard as we could. But the Canucks took the third game 4–0 in a battle where we let them get under our skin. I got hammered by Tim Hunter behind the Canucks goal and then was tossed out after the brawl that ensued. We never regained our composure.

In Vancouver, Gino Odjick was all over me on every shift. Clark didn't take too kindly to that. Odjick was playing on a line with Pavel Bure. During one of the faceoffs, Clark went up to Bure and said, "If Gino touches Gilmour one more time, I'm going to kill *you*." That was Wendel's philosophy: "If you're going after our best player, we're going after your best player."

Bure passed the message on.

Kirk McLean blanked us for the second straight time as we fell 2–0 in Game 4—and we were suddenly a game away from elimination.

Burns had lunch by the hotel pool with Clark, Todd Gill and me on our day off between Games 4 and 5. We knew we were in tough and that it was going to take everything we had to pull us back into the series. He wanted to lean on the team's leaders to get everyone on the same page.

"We're all looking for answers," Burns said. "We just have to come out of this and win a game in their building."

This was our last shot. We just had to win one game and bring it home.

We obviously felt nervous, being in such a deep hole with our season on the line. But we were also confident. We really believed that we could pull ourselves back into the series. And for a while, it looked like we'd found the performance we needed as we built a three-goal lead in the first period. If we could win that game, we were heading back home to the Gardens. Maybe we could pull this off, after all. But the Canucks came back, scoring three straight goals in the second period to tie it up, and we ended up going to overtime. Our hopes stayed alive through the first extra period, but that week from hell, where we were unable to muster a single win on the road, ended 14 seconds into the second overtime period, when Greg Adams scored. We lost 4–3, and just like that, our season was over.

Once again, we'd reached the threshold of the Stanley Cup Final—and fallen just short.

On the four-and-a-half-hour flight home, there was plenty of time to think about how disappointing the loss was. That's the hardest thing. You really feel the pain of losing, more than the bumps and bruises—because you're always going to have those. But mentally, you're not ready to shut it down. You know you had one shot with the guys in that room, you went to war with them, and now it's done. You get back home and have your team meetings, and you have your year-end parties with your buddies. But after that, you don't know what comes next. You don't know what's going to happen next year. You don't know who's coming back. Contracts expire. Guys will get traded. Changes are going to be made. It's a difficult feeling.

There is only one outcome to a season that leaves you satisfied. I felt it once. All I wanted was to drink from that Cup again. Nothing else would do.

17

"HOCKEY STAR"

I WAS ON A GOLF COURSE in Kingston when I heard the news. It was draft day, in late June of 1994.

It was actually a reporter who told me—he'd called the course, looking for a comment from me on "the trade." I didn't know what he was talking about.

Wendel Clark had been traded, he told me.

I was as shocked as everyone else in Toronto when I heard the news.

I knew nothing was ever certain. I knew there was no way we'd always keep the squad together. But this was the last thing I expected. Clark? Our captain? The heart and soul of our team? How do you replace a guy like Wendel?

But after we lost two years in a row in the conference final, our management felt a significant change was necessary. We had come close, but not close enough. Something had to give.

In addition to Clark, Toronto was sending defenceman Sylvain Lefebvre, a collegiate player named Landon Wilson and our first-round pick, 22nd overall, in the 1994 draft to the Quebec Nordiques. In return, we were getting centreman Mats Sundin, defenceman Garth Butcher, forward Todd Warriner and the 10th-overall pick in the '94 draft. The key players were Clark and Sundin, and in hindsight, it turned out to be a very good deal for the Leafs. But it also signalled a changing of the guard for our organization. At just 23 years old, the six-foot, five-inch Swedish star represented the Leafs' future.

It was another Cliff Fletcher blockbuster. Coming off his fourth season in Quebec, Sundin was young, he was big and he was good. He'd only been in the league four years, but I'd played against him enough to know he was going to be a star.

At the same time, it was tough to see Wendel go.

The guys got together and had a going-away party for Clark at a restaurant downtown. I never asked him how he felt. I think we all just kind of knew it was weird. We knew it was the end of an era, in a way. Clark had been a number one pick, and he'd been a constant presence on the team through some really awful seasons before these two great years we'd just been through. The general feeling was "Why would we do this? Why would we trade this guy?" Looking back, it's clear just how good Sundin was. But at the time, we didn't know that.

All we knew was that a lot of character had just left our locker room.

As I said, we'd come close, but not close enough. And man, some people in Toronto took losing hard. One night shortly after we were knocked out by Vancouver, I heard noise coming from the front lawn. I looked out the window and saw three kids, maybe 20 years old, sitting on the lawn with a case of beer. They were clearly smashed, and they were yelling at the house—"You guys suck! What a bunch of losers!"

I crawled out a window onto the roof of my garage.

"Please, I don't want to call the cops," I said. "Take this elsewhere."

"You suck, Gilmour!" they shouted. And then they started throwing bottles at the house. It was insane.

"All right," I said. "I'll make the call."

I went downstairs and grabbed a baseball bat and a carton of eggs, and I returned to the roof of the garage.

"Okay, I've called the cops, so you can just stay there until they arrive," I said. "But here's the thing—you have about 10 seconds to get off my lawn, because after that these eggs are coming down."

And I started firing the eggs at them. They jumped up, covered in yolk, as though they were going to come at me.

I had the bat in my left hand.

"Hey, I'm available," I shouted. "All three of you . . ."

I wasn't going to hit anybody with the bat, obviously, but the threat worked. They took off into the night.

I climbed back into the house, shaking my head. I was going to have to move *again.* It was frustrating. But after those instances—with lingerie left at our door, the threatening letters, and now these punks on my lawn—it was just too much. I knew then that we weren't long for living just off a public street like that. After those incidents, it was like there was nothing else we could do but move back to a condo and hide out. Once again, I had our real estate agent looking for a new place.

At 31 years old, I was literally telling kids to get off my lawn. I felt like an old man! And well, let's be honest, I was getting up there in hockey years. While my body had recovered well over the off-season from the constant beating of the long playoff run in 1993, just a year later I was starting to feel the long, hard miles adding up.

I knew I still had plenty of hockey left in me, but it certainly wasn't going to get any easier.

That summer, I started working out with my pal Gary Roberts, who was living in the city during the summers and had a trainer that he liked. We worked out in Etobicoke, somewhere close to the airport. It didn't last long—only a couple of weeks—because I ripped my biceps doing a pull-up. So that was it; I quit. I was done working out with Roberts!

I was particular about the way I worked out. I lifted weights, but never heavy ones. Any time I actually put on muscle and weight, it just slowed me down. There was always this idea that I needed to be heavier, but the extra bulk never made me any better! Putting on eight to 10 pounds actually hurt me. I just didn't feel the same. When I look back on it, it was always the conditioning that made me faster and stronger—running up and down that hill, constantly. On the ice, my job wasn't to be overpowering in the corners, or anything like that. It was to be quick out of the corner and make plays.

Over the summer of 1994, I finally decided to have my feet operated on. The bones on the top of my feet bowed upwards, and it caused terrible pain when I was skating. If you were to have watched our bench back then, you'd have noticed me untying my skates after every other shift and doing them back up before returning to the ice. My feet hurt that much.

The doctor told me I needed to have the bones shaved down. What a bad experience that was. I had to wear flip-flops for two weeks while the stitches and everything healed. I couldn't put skates on. I couldn't even wear shoes. It was brutal.

When I re-signed with the Leafs, we agreed that the Leafs would look for opportunities to market me with corporate sponsors. Things were handled differently in those days—I didn't have my own representative, so companies would approach the Leafs, and they'd present the idea to me. And I'd just say, "Yeah, I'll do it." It was a way to earn a little extra on top of my salary.

The first commercial I did was for Head & Shoulders shampoo. As it turned out, Amy's stepfather was in charge of lighting on the set. He kept mooning me every time I tried to do my lines so that I'd mess up. But it was good to have a familiar face. I was actually really nervous. You'd think those spots on "Coach's Corner" with Ron and Don would have prepared me for being in front of the camera, but this was different!

In the commercial, I'm introduced as "Doug Gilmour: Hockey Star." (That would have made a good business card.) I wore a suit in the ad and said I couldn't afford to have dandruff in front of the media, and that I used Head & Shoulders.

I nailed it! But the guys certainly gave me a hard time about that one.

The milk commercials were probably the best known. In the first one, two players are sitting in a locker room talking about me, and one says, "Hey, Dougieee, what's your secret?" in a French or Russian accent (it's hard to tell).

I turn around and say, "Hey, guys. Hard work, balanced diet, variety—including milk. Cold, refreshing milk!" And then I take a sip from a glass of milk as the camera pans down to my legs, which look like they belong to a cow.

That commercial was *quite* a scene. When I showed up for the shoot, they handed me a Speedo. I changed into it, and when I came out there was a guy on one side of me and a girl on the other, telling me they had to shave my legs. And they did; they lathered me up and shaved me down. Then came *three hours* of painting my silky-smooth, hairless legs to look like a cow's. A lot of people didn't realize that those legs were painted on. Every time we did a new take for the commercial, I'd turn around and my Leafs sweater would smear the paint. During breaks, I'd have to take the sweater off to keep it from ruining the cow legs. Picture me on the set, meeting the people from the Ontario Milk Marketing Board, with nothing but a Speedo on with the legs of a cow, and I'm greeting them with one hand over my crotch.

The commercial was such a fun thing to do. The best part about it was that after it started airing, I'd be in a grocery store or walking down the street, and four- or five-year-olds with their parents would stop and recognize me. They'd say, "Hey, that's the milk guy!" It wasn't "the hockey player"—it was "the milk guy." I loved that.

But I got even more shit from my teammates than I did after the first commercial—because, well, my legs aren't very big. And then I'd have teammates saying, "Hey, Dougieee! Hey, Dougieee!" all the time. The chirps were pretty good.

When we arrived for training camp in September 1994, everyone knew the NHL season was in jeopardy. The league said it wanted to "tax" teams that had higher payrolls, but we players saw it as a salary cap, and that wasn't going to work for us. We wanted to continue playing under the old collective bargaining agreement while a new one was negotiated, but the league wanted us to accept a new agreement that would ultimately rein in our salaries.

We knew all summer that the dispute was going to boil over, but we were practising in hopes that a resolution would come in time to start the season. When that didn't happen, we knew we weren't going to miss just a couple of weeks, as we had in April of 1992. We were going to be locked out for a while. The National Hockey League Players' Association had prepared us for the possibility that we would lose an entire season.

Training camp was held at a facility north of Toronto called Teen Ranch. We were on the ice for about an hour one afternoon with the assistant coaches when Burns came out to the bench and blew a whistle.

"You guys are done," he said. "It's a lockout."

We had no idea when we'd be back.

During the stoppage, we were only on the ice about once a week. We weren't allowed into the Gardens, so we'd just rent ice somewhere. The NHLPA organized a four-on-four showcase tournament in Hamilton for the fans and to keep the players busy. Lots of stars participated, including Patrick Roy, Luc Robitaille, Brett Hull and Joe Sakic. All the proceeds went to charity. It was more like an alumni game—we weren't going 100 per cent, but it was fun to get out and play in front of the fans again.

The truth was, a lot of us just really wanted to get out on the ice. Every day, somebody would stop you on the street, asking about the "strike." We kept having to explain that it wasn't a strike, it was a lockout. But that distinction wasn't clear to many people. We wanted to play, but at the same time, we had to stick together. We knew how important it all was. But there were a lot of questions, and at some points I just wanted to get out of Dodge.

We had a series of meetings after the four-on-four showcase, and it was clear that we weren't going to be playing until at least Christmas, if we were going to play at all. When that happened, we had to figure out whether we wanted to stick around town and wait or look for someplace to play. Guys started to call their agents and tell them to look for opportunities overseas.

I ended up signing with Rapperswil-Jona of National League A in Switzerland. I was paid $10,000 during the six weeks I was there, but it cost me almost $8,000 to travel and live. I only played nine games, but it was definitely the "vacation" I needed. Around the same time, Wayne Gretzky organized a European tour of games featuring an invitation-only lineup. We played in places like Helsinki, Stockholm, Bern, Düsseldorf and Milan.

The league and the players' association finally reached an agreement to end the lockout in early January of 1995. It had become clear that losing the entire season would be a huge detriment to the league. We managed to emerge from the negotiations without a salary cap. We'd only get to play a 48-game season, but at least we were back.

It was weird to be back in a Leafs sweater without Wendel Clark. I was given the captaincy, which meant a lot to me. I was so proud to wear the *C* on the blue and white sweater. And Sundin was obviously a great addition to the franchise.

When Mats was first traded to Toronto, Cliff asked me to take him out to dinner. We went out to a theatre show afterwards. It was a great first date!

Mats was a quiet, serious guy. He'd come out for the occasional beer back then, but most of the time he'd end up back home, resting. He was a natural leader. And he was tough. He played harder than people thought he did. He was six-foot-five, 230 pounds! At 170, I could only dream of being that big. And yet, for a power forward he also had remarkable skill. And he was so consistent.

But the team didn't really get a chance to gel on the ice during that shortened season. After two strong years, we finished fourth in the Central Division with a record of 21–19–8 and limped into the playoffs. I suffered two herniated discs that put me on the sidelines for the final month. It was horrible. It was the worst pain I'd felt in my life. I could barely bend down to tie up my skates. It ached even when I was lying in bed. At 32 years old, I was starting to feel more like 60. I managed to miss only four regular-season games, but I scored just 10 goals and 33 points in 44 games.

Despite the pain, I was in uniform for our playoff series against Chicago. The Blackhawks had finished only three points ahead of us in the standings but had scored 21 more goals while allowing 31 fewer, so we were the clear underdogs. Even so, we battled hard, opening the series with two wins in their barn. But we were overmatched and the Blackhawks fought their way back, winning the next three games. We led Game 6 with a score of 4–1 early in the third period, but they came back again to send it into overtime. We fought off elimination with an overtime win, forcing a final, deciding game back in Chicago, which the Blackhawks took 5–2, ending our season.

It was a difficult result to swallow. After the series, I was off for surgery and a summer of back rehab, as I vowed to do everything I could to get back on the ice. But in many ways, that lockout season was the beginning of the end of my time as a Maple Leaf.

Still, I enjoyed spending time away from the rink with the team. That summer, a bunch of us went on a bit of a cross–Eastern Ontario tour, playing in a couple of charity golf tournaments. We travelled in a big Winnebago. It was a fun few days. Tie Domi, who had joined the Leafs from Winnipeg that year, was with us. He brought along this brand new pair of Nike sandals and these fancy new clubs. I decided I needed to play a bit of a prank on him. So, on the way down to my parents' place after a tournament in Kingston, I called my dad and told him I needed him to go and pick me up some gold spray paint. He had no idea what I was up to, but he helped me out. The next day, at a tournament in Brockville, Tie pulled the sandals out of his bag and freaked out. They were painted gold. He was so pissed off at me. It was great.

But if he thought the prank was over, he was mistaken. Not so. There were about 100 or so people watching me chip and putt on the practice green while Tie's group was teeing off. I had just chipped a shot when I heard Tie yelling from the tee blocks: "Gilmour! I'm going to get you, you little bastard!" I'd also spray-painted the head of his fancy driver. It was an instant classic. But the *coup de grâce* came as we approached his foursome on the fairway while they were about to putt on the first hole. Tie pulled the cover off his putter—and he must have had the Midas touch, because, damn it, his putter was shimmering gold, too.

"Gilmour!" he hollered. He was livid.

I nearly fell over laughing.

18

END OF AN ERA

As soon as I got the call from Cliff Fletcher, I knew it was over.

In February of 1997, I was 33 years old and in the last year of my contract with the Leafs before I could exercise my player's option. I was prepared to take it. In fact, I had considered signing on for three more years before possibly retiring.

The two years leading up to that call had not been the best. In 1995–96, our team had another rough season. We finished third in the Central Division, with a 34–36–12 record, and once again lost in the first round of the playoffs—this time to the St. Louis Blues. I picked up 72 points in 81 games while still playing with my nagging back injury. My good friend Kirk

Muller had joined the team in the second half of the season, which was nice. But we just couldn't recapture the magic we'd had as a team during those two runs to the conference final in 1993 and 1994. The biggest blow came when Pat Burns was fired in February following an eight-game losing streak. I was pissed off because there were rumours that some of the guys in the locker room were happy to see him go. That might have been true, but Pat had been great to us. We owed him so much.

Pat called me from the road while he was driving to Quebec after he was canned. He thanked me for our years together. I thought of that first meeting we had together, at Filmores, back when this journey began. It seemed so long ago.

Away from the rink, life was going great. Amy and I had married in the summer of 1995 and had moved to Etobicoke after living in a downtown condo called the Polo Club for a couple of years. Our first son, Jake, was born in August 1996. In fact, Amy was pregnant with Jake when we filmed a commercial for the Ontario Milk Marketing Board together. No leg shaving was required this time—they made up special nylons. The ad features us dancing elegantly together. I am dressed in a suit, with my Leafs sweater overtop. As a voiceover asks what the "Gilmours' secret" is, I pull up my suit pants to reveal my cow legs, and Amy does the same with her red dress. Then we do a jig to some bluegrass music before Amy takes a sip of milk. "What taste!" she says. "Why, thank you, Amy," I reply. I got some shit for that one, too, but it was a lot of fun.

Now, at 33 years old, with a newborn son and a daughter who

was already almost a teenager, I was in a unique place in my life. I loved being a dad, and I was thrilled to welcome Jake into our lives.

On the ice, I was back up to a point-per-game player in 1996–97. I was skating on a line with Tie Domi and Wendel Clark, who had returned to the Leafs after spending the previous two seasons with the Nordiques and then the Islanders. I was happy to have Clark back in the locker room, but it wasn't really our team anymore. Mike Murphy had taken over as head coach. We were on our way to a last-place finish in our division, and frustrations were boiling over. We were inconsistent. We were finding ways to lose. We were even being booed at home. It was embarrassing. I was vocal about my frustration with that situation in the press.

There was speculation in the media that I wanted out of Toronto. I didn't like that, but I had to bite my tongue. Often, you'd want to say something to one of the writers who put something stupid about you in the paper. But it just wasn't worth it. You just had to have a thick skin.

The fact is, I didn't want to go anywhere. But Cliff and I had discussed the possibility of a trade earlier in the season. He knew his own job was on the line because the Leafs' majority owner, Steve Stavro, was looking to build something new. Regardless, Cliff didn't want to trade me. And he told me he wouldn't without my approval. I appreciated that. I really did. But I also knew that I only wanted to play for a franchise that wanted me. Just like in Calgary, if a team didn't want me anymore, then I'd rather be somewhere else. If Stavro didn't want me, I didn't want to be there. It had nothing to do with the team, and nothing to do with the fans. I just wanted to play where I was wanted. I felt I still had a lot of quality hockey left in me.

As trade rumours began to crop up in the local media, it was hard on my daughter; some of her classmates started bugging her about it. She was only about 12 at the time, and living in Oakville with her mom. "Your dad's no good anymore," they taunted. It crushed me when Maddie told me about it.

"Dad, how are you doing?" she asked me over the phone.

"Real good," I said.

"A lot of kids here are saying you're going to get traded because you're no good," she said sadly.

"Well, let's put it this way," I said. "I'm going to get traded because other teams want me."

At that moment, I have to admit, part of me wanted to make sure I wasn't traded to another Canadian team. I was sick of the press and the pressure. It was getting to me. Pro athletes often try to pretend that they're not paying attention to the media. But we know what everyone is saying. You try to avoid the papers or the radio or television, but someone will point it out to you. My dad would often call me up and tell me what so-and-so said, and I'd have to say, "Dad, I don't care! That's why I don't read that shit!"

That was the underlying context that followed me throughout those two seasons leading up to my trade out of Toronto.

I did my best to ignore the talk and maintain my focus on hockey, but finally my temper boiled over. We were practising at St. Michael's Arena, and assistant coach Mike Kitchen said something to me I didn't like. It was something harmless, like "We've got to get better." But I was already on edge because I knew I was likely to get traded. As soon as he made the remark, I hurled my stick across the ice. It helicoptered about 30 feet through the air. Everyone just stopped. It didn't go near Mike, but it was certainly aimed in his direction. I felt bad. It wasn't his fault I was so upset. He didn't even know that I knew about the possibility of getting moved. He was just trying to generate some motivation. When I skated over to pick up the stick, he looked at me and said, "That's how you shoot these days. You know that, right?"

I could only shake my head. "Yeah," I said. "You're right."

That's what assistant coaches are great at. They're like buffers. They're the ones you can get mad at, without it going all the way to the head coach. Sometimes, you just have to vent. You have to show a little emotion. Guys like Mike could handle it. I could curse at him, let off steam, and just as quickly calm down and apologize. He'd understand. We're all on the same page. We're all frustrated. The coaches want to win as much as the players do.

A couple weeks later, while we were in Vancouver in the middle of February, Cliff called me. The trade deadline was just a couple of weeks away. He said he needed to talk to me in person. I went over to his hotel room and sat down. He and

I had a great relationship, and I always knew he was being straight with me.

"Here's the deal," Cliff said. "They're not going to re-sign you. And I'm pretty much on the outs as well."

Once again, he said he didn't want to trade me. But there were already offers on the table.

"Cliff, if the ownership doesn't want me, then it doesn't make any sense to keep me," I said. "Try to salvage your job. Trade me for some young players."

I told Cliff I wanted to play for a team that really wanted me. One with good management and good coaches, and a chance to win the Stanley Cup. I also told him I wanted to play somewhere in the States but close to Toronto. After spending so much time away from home for so many years, I hadn't had the chance to be the kind of father I wanted to be to Maddie. Now, with a new young family and Maddie close by, I didn't want to jeopardize that again.

In hindsight, my request probably cost the Leafs the best deal they could have made for me. Cliff told me which teams were interested, and the first one was Vancouver. The Canucks' general manager, Pat Quinn—Cliff's old friend—was considering sending young prospect Markus Naslund to Toronto for me. At the time, he was only 23 years old and was really just coming into his own, in only his fourth season in the league. He would go on to become a focal point of the Canucks franchise—a team captain, a first-team all-star, and even a Lester Pearson Award winner as the players' choice of

MVP. In 2002–03 he put up 48 goals and 104 points. Naslund would have had a big impact with the Leafs.

I told Cliff I didn't want to go to Vancouver. It wasn't because of the team, but because of the distance from southern Ontario and the long flights. It was just too far away from where I needed to be in my life.

Cliff understood. He said there were three other teams interested in me: the Florida Panthers, the Philadelphia Flyers and the New Jersey Devils. I told him I was okay with any of the three, and then I left him to do his job. I didn't know where, but I knew I was going somewhere soon. My time as a Maple Leaf was done.

That night, we beat Vancouver 6–5. My "A" game was back. I scored a goal each in the first and second period. I knew I was leaving and I was determined to prove my worth. It was my old, familiar mentality: You don't want me? Well, then, fuck you. I'll prove you wrong.

We played the next night in Edmonton, then flew to Montreal to finish off a six-game road swing before heading home. We had a four-day break after the Montreal game. If there was going to be a trade, that seemed as likely a time as any.

A couple of days after the Habs game, we took a school bus over to St. Mike's Arena for a team practice. Before I got on the bus, Cliff pulled me aside and told me a deal was about to be made but that he wanted me to go to practice anyway. The media weren't aware yet. Assistant coach Mike Kitchen ran the practice, and I just went through the motions, because I knew I was on my way out.

After practice, Cliff came and found me in the locker room. He told me I was heading to the New Jersey Devils. I told him I was heading to Oakville to pick up my daughter so I could tell her before the news broke and she learned about it at school. On the way, I got a call from Lou Lamoriello, the Devils' general manager, who told me they'd have a plane come and get me to take me to New Jersey that night.

On my way to Oakville, I learned that I was heading to the Devils with my good friend Dave Ellett, in exchange for three young players: Steve Sullivan, Jason Smith and Alyn McCauley, who was still in junior. It was already on the radio. I took Maddie out of school and brought her back to my place and explained what was happening before someone else told her. The possibility of a trade had been in the news, but everyone was just speculating about which team I'd go to. I wanted to tell her myself.

"I'm not that far away," I said. "And it's only three months, and then I'll be back in the summertime."

I found it frustrating that I had to worry about my daughter finding out from someone else. You try to keep the outside noise to a minimum, but there is really only so much you can do. It's easy to forget that people have families—that they have lives beyond the rink.

I didn't give a press conference. I was too busy getting everything ready and spending time with my daughter. Ellett took the bullet for me and spoke to the press that day. I was watching on TV. "I'm just happy they threw Doug in the deal," he said, with a smile. I started howling at home. He always had a great sense of humour.

Eventually, the media found me at our house in Etobicoke. I knew I had to say something. I couldn't just ignore it, even though that's really what I wanted to do. I told them I could give them 10 minutes.

I was never good with this stuff. I didn't like being in front of the cameras. I didn't like sharing my emotions. And I had a lot of them. Toronto had meant so much to me. The fans were incredible. The organization had been great. It was where I had played the best hockey of my life. I thought of my old teammates, and of Pat Burns—and of all the battles. The blood, sweat and tears. I thought about how close we'd come, and how now, it was all over.

I also thought about my parents. They had worked so hard to help me fulfil my dreams—with all their time and patience and money spent. They had such a great time coming down to see me play at the Gardens. It meant everything to them. My dad would talk to me after every game, giving me his thoughts on what I'd done wrong, or how the team could improve. Annoying as it could be, I loved every minute of it. "Okay, thanks, Don," I said, joking that he was just like his old friend Don Cherry. Even at that point in my career, I spoke to my dad pretty much every single day.

I called them and told them the news myself. It was a hard conversation to have. Like I said, it's so easy to forget about the family side of these things. They were hurt and sad. They'd loved my time in Toronto so much. But there was nothing we could do. Now they would not be jumping in the car anymore and coming to see me in Toronto. They would have to just sit back and watch the games on TV again. Years later, that's the part that I look back on, and I wish that I could have had that back and played a few more years in Toronto.

All of those thoughts swirled through my head as I stood there in front of the cameras, on my lawn, and did my best to say thank you to Toronto. This was my home. I knew that much. And I was going to miss it. It was hard. It's always hard.

The Leafs were heading in a new direction, too. They wouldn't make the playoffs, and at the end of the season, Cliff Fletcher was let go—just as he'd expected. The Leafs would hire Ken Dryden to replace him. A year later, they'd bring in Pat Quinn.

But I wasn't going to be part of that. I was boarding a chartered plane at Pearson International Airport with Dave Ellett, heading south to New Jersey.

19

A NEW BEGINNING

When Dave Ellett and I arrived around midnight to meet our new team, Lou Lamoriello was there to greet us. I'd always had a great deal of respect for Lou. He is a gentleman and one of the most respected figures in the game. But he is also incredibly old-school, so I wasn't surprised when he told me he wanted me to wear number 9 because—shades of Tom Watt—he didn't like having high numbers on the roster.

"Lou, that's my past," I told him. "I want 93."

He was great about it, though. He understood.

The next morning, I joined everyone on the team for the first time, for a mandatory team breakfast. The guys didn't even say hi to me. They just came up and starting asking what number I was wearing. Turns out they had a bet going to see what I'd end up with. Only Martin Brodeur predicted correctly that I'd be wearing number 93. I think he won $1,000.

Ellett and I both moved into a hotel for the remainder of the season. We didn't have our cars down there yet, so we took a shuttle bus between the hotel and the Meadowlands Arena. After nearly a decade of playing in Canada, between Calgary and Toronto, I was used to most people around rinks recognizing me. When my car finally arrived in New Jersey, I drove it into the parking lot at the Meadowlands and pulled up to the security gate. The guard inside stopped me. I didn't have my pass yet and my car wasn't registered.

"Can I help you?" he asked.

"I'm a player," I said.

"What's your name?"

"Gilmour."

"Never heard of you," he said. "Park over there."

He pointed to a lot about a half mile down the road. I had to walk all the way into the rink. A lot can change when you go from one market to another.

It wasn't all that bad, though. In Calgary and Toronto for eight years, I was the focus of constant attention. I'd certainly miss that at times, but for now, in New Jersey, I could walk the streets and no one would know who I was. I could go anywhere I wanted. There's a big difference in the hockey culture between Canada and the States.

...

I was joining a very good team in the Devils. We had one of the best goalies ever to play in the NHL and a solid roster overall. My old linemate Dave Andreychuk had been traded to New Jersey a season earlier, so it was nice to be reunited with him. Along with him we had forwards like John MacLean, Bobby Holik and Bill Guerin. And on defence we had two future Hall of Famers in Scott Stevens and Scott Niedermayer.

On top of that, Jacques Lemaire was one of the smartest coaches I ever had. He involved everybody in the game plan. He made sure everybody on the team sat in on the special-teams meetings, even if they weren't going to play on the power-play or penalty-killing units. There'd be a TV and he'd say, "Okay, this is what we're doing." That way, everybody was prepared, regardless of what might happen. I loved it because nobody felt left out. We were a team. At the end of those meetings, he always showed us what he called "Da Faces." It was a sort of blooper reel showing guys picking their noses on the bench or waving to people in the stands. He'd put this reel on 15 to 20 minutes before we went out for a warm-up, and we'd all be howling.

On the ice, we played the neutral-zone trap, which I think of as hockey's version of Red Rover. We'd sit there and wait for the other team to come to us—and then we'd go on the attack. It was like setting a trap. Sometimes, we really didn't have to work that hard. We'd press for maybe 15 minutes tops one night, and then seven the next. You didn't sweat that much. We just sat back: "Come on . . . come to us." Lemaire would work us hard in practice because we needed to keep our conditioning up. We'd go into a game and win it 3–1. In my eyes, we should have won it 7–1. I mean, we passed up scoring chances! But it worked.

We finished first overall in the Eastern Conference that spring, but we lost to the New York Rangers in the second round of the playoffs.

At the end of the season, my option year was coming up. In hopes of avoiding arbitration, Lou offered me a new four-year deal worth between $5 million and $5.5 million a season. I couldn't make any more than Stevens or Brodeur, because they were the stars of the team, but it was still a great offer. I spoke with my agent, Larry Kelly, about it, and we decided that I had to play out my option and pursue free agency after the upcoming season. It had taken a long time to get there, and I had to at least take a shot at getting as much as I could on the open market, because it was very likely that my next contract would be my last. The NHLPA was also putting a lot of pressure on players to file for free agency, because it helps keep salaries healthy.

When I ended up going to arbitration to determine what I'd be paid that final season in New Jersey, I was an elder statesman in the NHL, and Lou treated me with a lot of respect. Before we went, he let me know we were going to be there all day and that there would be someone speaking on the team's behalf—and that representative would say things in the hearing that I wouldn't like.

"Listen, this is arbitration," he said. "Don't listen to everything that goes on here."

He was right. It was pretty tough. They started out by asking why I'd make this much money, when so-and-so—I think it was Pierre Turgeon—was making this much less and was a much better player than I was. *Ouch.*

I scribbled on a notepad and pushed it over to my agent: *If they think he's a better player than I am, tell them to trade me for him.*

Larry just looked at me and shook his head. It was best for me to stay out of it.

After about four hours, we had a break for lunch. I was walking around outside and Lou came over to see me again.

"Doug, please understand," he said. "This is just arbitration."

That's what I love about Lou. I respect him to this day. And I can call him up tomorrow and ask him a question, or for a favour, or anything. He is first class. Cliff Fletcher was the same way.

Was I happy about hearing the things they said to make their case? No. You don't want to hear people debating your value like that. But it was an interesting process to sit through. They came prepared with their ideas of what I was worth, and we came with ours. It was a much different time. We didn't have access to all of the analytical tools they do today, for one thing. I actually looked at the back of Pat LaFontaine's hockey card and compared our numbers—games, goals, assists, points, penalty minutes. He was making more than we were asking for, so I gave it to my agent. We had to go with the information we had at the time.

Five days after the hearing, the arbitrator's ruling was delivered. I had been making about $2.6 million in U.S. dollars, and now I was being bumped up to about $3.2 million. It was a fine raise for one season. When it was all said and done, neither side came away from the process with any regrets.

That summer, I bought a cottage on Loughborough Lake, right next to the place my parents owned. It was nice to be able to buy something near them, so we could all spend more time together in the off-season. It was great, too, because a bunch of my friends from the game also bought places on the lake just north of Kingston. Dan Aykroyd still had his place. Kirk Muller, Dave Ellett and Wendel Clark all had properties there by now. We'd all head up there in the summers and go into town to skate and train in the mornings, and then go relax on the lake in the afternoon and have a bonfire at night. We'd be out for a campfire until about 1 a.m., and then back to the rink at 6:30 the next morning. It was the perfect way to spend the summer. It kind of felt like being a teenager again. It was nice to be able to take some time to spend with family and friends, away from all the pressures of the game.

Sometimes Dad and I would go fishing together in bass season. We'd challenge our neighbours to see who could catch the most. Dad was really impatient, which isn't a great quality for a fisherman. We'd be in one spot for about 15 minutes, and he'd reel in his line and move to another. The neighbours would laugh at us from their boat across the lake. We never won.

Other times, Dad and I would set out at around seven in the morning, and we'd crack open the first beer by 7:30. We'd come back a few hours—and several beers—later. We had a great time out there on the water together. I think of those times often when I look out at the lake. I wouldn't trade those mornings we shared together for anything.

When I returned to New Jersey that fall, my first paycheque was higher than I expected, because of the arbitration ruling. It was for about $130,000. After I picked it up, I went to a local bar with some of the guys from the team. Before I went in, I tossed out some of the garbage in my car. I had been sitting in the bar with the guys for about a half hour when I got a funny feeling. I checked my pockets and realized I didn't have my paycheque on me. I ran out to my car and looked around and couldn't find it. Then it hit me. I walked over to the trash can and opened it up. There was my paycheque, still in its envelope, sitting on top of a big heap of trash. *Shit.* It was unbelievable. I was lucky.

That season, I suffered one of the scariest and probably most painful injuries that I ever experienced. We were playing in Philadelphia. The Flyers' Eric Desjardins took a backhand to dump the puck in and it hit me right in the eye.

I went down right away. Of all the injuries I sustained—losing teeth, hurting my knee, shoulder surgery, back surgery—this was the worst. It felt like a sharp needle going through my eye. Thank God it was only a backhand. They put a patch on it at the rink, and then we bused an hour and a half back to New Jersey, where I went right to the hospital. I was there for four days, unsure if I'd be able to see out of my eye again. I was 35 years old, wondering how I was going to deal with being blind in one eye. It was the first time I was really scared after an injury. My career was in jeopardy. I didn't know what was going to happen. I was there by myself because I'd just been traded and Amy and Jake, who was about a year and a half, were still in Toronto. I called home all the time to give updates, but really, all I could do was wait.

They had to wait until the swelling went down to take the patch off. Everything was blurry when they finally took it off, which was a relief because at least the eye was seeing something. After a bit of time, my vision cleared.

I was okay to play about a week and a half later. I had full vision, so that was the biggest thing. I wore a visor for about two periods of my first game back, before I couldn't handle it anymore. I just couldn't do it. It didn't feel right. It was this old-school mentality that I couldn't shake. In hindsight, yeah, that was dumb. Today, I look at all of these kids coming out of junior, having worn a full face mask for their entire lives, and then taking them off and replacing them with visors. Part of me thinks they should just keep the cages on. It would be a safer idea. Throughout my career, I had pretty much all of my front teeth knocked out. I had a bridge put in, and then that got knocked out, too. So a lot of the time I played with missing teeth. It certainly played into the clichés about hockey being a tough sport, but I'm not sure it did much else. I wasn't wearing the bridge when I played in New Jersey. Around that time, I remember looking at a recent hockey card that had a photo of me with my teeth out. I looked like I was 47 years old instead of in my early 30s.

"Oh God," I thought. "I'm putting my teeth back in!"

To be honest, I didn't really wear shoulder pads, either. I'd put on the flimsiest pair I could find. And I would cut the padding out of my pants. The trainers never realized what I was doing until they'd handle my equipment and say, "What's this, Doug?" My gloves also had to be loose. I couldn't control the puck with tight-fitting gloves. My skates had to be loose, too. I couldn't wear them right out of the box. I didn't like for them to be too stiff. So basically, I would have played with no gear on if I could have!

A lot of the younger guys coming in were used to playing with bigger, more protective gear. I could never do that. It was something I had to live with.

You're going to get hurt in the game, no matter what. There will always be bumps and bruises along the way. It's going to hurt. Still, you're going to play through it. But when something major, like your back or your knee, gets injured, you can't play the same way anymore. You try your best, of course. You take a painkiller here and there, but eventually, that's not good for your stomach. I wouldn't be able to eat after taking painkillers, which is worse than playing with pain. So I actually stopped taking pills altogether. That's not to say I'm especially tough or anything like that. I think it's just that you learn to tolerate pain. It was part of the game—at least mine. Pain was a constant presence.

After that eye injury in New Jersey, I became acutely aware of how all these injuries might affect me later on in life. Thankfully, I wasn't blind, but there were so many other injuries that would take a toll.

Around the same time, I started to worry that other parts of me were starting to go, too. During a road trip in Pittsburgh, I went out and had a bite to eat one night with the team at the hotel and then ended up on the patio of a Señor Frog's bar to have a couple beers before curfew. The bar was maybe a five-minute cab ride from the hotel. I had a big dinner and probably had about 10 beers. I got up to walk back to the hotel and I let out a fart—or at least, I *thought* I had. It turned out that I had shit my pants. I couldn't get in the cab now! I just ducked around the corner while the other guys took a cab without me.

I had to walk all the way back to the hotel. The guys had been back for about 20 minutes by this point. When I got to the hotel, there were autograph seekers waiting for us in the lobby. I had to a pull a "Not today, guys" and walk right past them as quickly as possible. I went to my room and jumped right in the shower with my dress pants on.

The problem was, I only had one suit!

I had to call someone downstairs to get my pants dried for the morning. The hotel employee came to collect them. He walked into the bathroom and stumbled backward.

"Geez, did somebody shit their pants, man?" he said.

It was embarrassing. They took my pants and got them dried, but the next day they were all wrinkled. I skipped the mandatory breakfast and went right to the rink so no one would see me.

That year, in 1997–98, we once again finished first in the Eastern Conference with 107 points. Despite being sidelined with the eye injury, I still picked up 53 points in 63 games, finishing third in team scoring behind Bobby Holik and Scott Niedermayer. We still played a suffocating neutral-zone trap that shut down our opponents—making it especially hard to score against us, given that we had Marty in net. We gave up the fewest goals in the NHL, with 166.

We were legitimate Stanley Cup contenders heading into the playoffs. But the eighth-seeded Ottawa Senators beat us in six games in the first round of the playoffs. It was a huge upset and a bitter end to a promising season. The Devils were in the midst of building something great. It just wasn't clear whether I'd be part of it.

After we lost, Lou came and saw me. He told me that the team understood that I intended to test the free agency market, but that I would definitely hear from them. They wanted to make me an offer to stay. That was great to hear.

When July 1 came around and I was officially a free agent, three teams were interested. True to his word, Lou made me an offer similar to the one he'd made before I chose to go to arbitration. It was tempting. Despite that early exit from the playoffs, I believed in what they had put together in New Jersey. I respected management and loved the organization. But there were options to consider. Besides the Devils, Tampa Bay and Chicago both made offers. Going to play for the Tampa Bay Lightning was an intriguing possibility because Terry Crisp was their coach and Phil Esposito was their general manager. I liked playing for Terry and had a lot of respect for Phil. Then there were the Blackhawks. I got a call from team management, informing me that Brett Hull was planning to sign with Chicago and they wanted me to come, too. The idea of playing with Brett was a big draw. They had also signed Paul Coffey and Mark Janssens. Chris Chelios, who'd won multiple Norris Trophies, and Bob Probert were there, too.

Chicago offered me $6 million a year for three years. It paid more per season but less overall than the four-year deal the Devils were offering. In the end, I agreed to the deal with Chicago. But two days later, Hull signed with the Dallas Stars. His deal with Chicago had fallen through, which was a big disappointment for me.

I don't like using hindsight to try to judge decisions I've made, but in this case I should have stayed in New Jersey. It probably would have worked out better for me over the next four or five years. They ended up winning the Cup two years later, in 2000. It would have been great to have been there to be part of that championship team, but again, I made a decision and I have to live with it. I was cheering for the Devils from the sidelines as they played for the Cup. I wanted them to win. I respected the hell out of the organization, and they deserved it.

In August of 1998, my second son, Tyson, was born. I was so thrilled to have another child with Amy. Our young family was on the move to Chicago, which was an incredible city with great fans. Years later, long after I'd left the Windy City, I'd stay in close contact with the friends I'd met there, and the place would always feel like home.

And it was a great Original Six organization to be part of. The Blackhawks were a fun team with some great veterans. I played left wing on a line with Tony Amonte, a 40-goal scorer, and Alexei Zhamnov, which was great. We were the top three scorers on the team that year.

There were about eight of us veterans on that team who would get together after games and chat over some beers when we were on the road. Our season wasn't going very well at all, and we knew we had to talk about it, rather than just giving in. It was also important to get together to talk about any issues in the locker room. You have to take care of that stuff right away, or it festers.

In our younger days, we would have done that at a bar. But we were getting too old to go out all the time, and team rules prevented us from drinking at the hotel bar. So, while we were en route to our next hotel, we'd call them up and have room service send about 100 beers up to one of our rooms and just charge it to one of our credit cards. At the end of the day, we'd all pile into the room—guys like Zhamnov, Amonte and Chelios—and sit up for about an hour and a half, having five or six beers each before shutting it down. Probert would be there, too, but he wasn't drinking at all.

It's the times like that you really miss when your career is over. Just hanging out with the boys, sharing some laughs and some beers, talking hockey. You don't really realize it at the time, but those are the good times.

And when you're struggling as a team, it's important to relax and have some fun. The game can get to your head too much sometimes, which makes it impossible to perform. Some of the best coaches would send the guys out as a group to grab some pizza or have some beers together when we were in a slump. While we were struggling in Chicago that season, we had three days off in Arizona during a road trip. We all went and played a round of golf and had a few beers on the course. After golfing, we all went out for a steak and some wine. We had practice the next morning at 11 a.m. We were pretty slow. About half an hour into practice, our coach, Dirk Graham, blew his whistle and called everyone in.

"Okay, boys," he said. "Who had five or more beers yesterday?"

At the time, my roommate was Danny Cleary, who was a rookie. I gave him a nod to put his hand up, too. About seven or eight of us did.

"Okay. You guys, off the ice," Graham said to us. "The rest of you guys are lying."

They had to skate for another half hour. He knew what we were up to. He just wanted us to know it. That was one thing about Dirk that I really liked.

On that same road trip, during a practice in Colorado, I pulled my old trick of shooting pucks at the coach's skates when they were doing laps to warm up with the guys. If you hit them just right as they're turning, it takes them right out. This time, during a shooting drill, I fired the puck from the other end of the ice at Graham—and the puck shattered the plastic piece holding his skate blade in place. I went down and did push-ups right away so he wouldn't see me. Meanwhile, he was flat on the ice with no blade, trying to figure out how his skate had shattered. I was trying my best not to laugh. End to end and I hit my target. It was the best shot I ever took.

The point is, you have to have fun, whether you're winning or losing.

It was a good thing we had fun off the ice, because we didn't have much fun on it that season. We finished third in the Central Division with 70 points and missed the playoffs. It was the first time I'd played an entire season with a team and we didn't make the post-season. The only other time I'd missed the playoffs in my career was the season when I was traded to Toronto.

I had to have back surgery that summer, which was just another indication that my battered body was breaking down. The family and I went back to the cottage on Loughborough Lake while I recovered. While we were there, Dan Aykroyd and his band were playing at a small pub at the end of the lake that we often frequented. All the usual guys were there—Dave Ellett, Wendel Clark, Kirk Muller. It ended up being a long night, and we brought the party back to my dock. We were having a great time, several beers in, when I decided I wanted to take a dip in the water. I walked up the edge and went to do a backwards plunge into the lake, about two months after I'd finished surgery. I landed flat on my back on something hard. I just lay there, confused, not knowing what the hell had happened. I could see stars. Was I dead?

Then my head cleared, and I realized I was just lying on my ass in the bottom of our boat, which I'd forgotten I'd tied up there. I went to see my physio guy a couple days later, and I told him I wasn't sure how, but I'd tweaked my back just a bit. I ended up having to see him several times a week just to get the scar tissue broken down again. Lesson learned: always look before you leap.

The second year of my deal with Chicago wasn't much better than the first. I was bumped back to the third line and saw my ice time go way down. So I was bitter. As the trade deadline approached we were still about 10 points out of the playoffs. That's when I was blindsided by something I didn't expect at all: I was traded to the Buffalo Sabres, along with J.P. Dumont, for Michal Grosek. The Blackhawks retained half my salary in the deal.

Buffalo wouldn't have been my first choice of places to go, but it was much closer to home than Chicago. And the team had some talent.

I've met a lot of interesting characters between the pipes through the years, but Dominik Hasek—well, he was a different guy, even by goalie standards. I don't know if I've ever met someone as competitive as he was. In practice, you had to try your hardest to score on him all the time, or he'd get pissed off at you. If you were 20 feet away, he'd want you to take a full slapshot on him. If you scored, he'd be ready to throw his stick at you. But that's what made him so good. He hated to be scored on, regardless of the situation. And he was unpredictable. If you came in on a breakaway, one day he'd stand up; the next day he'd slide right at you. It messed with your head! Hasek played on his own terms, and he was one of the greatest goalies ever to play the game because of it.

The Sabres had scorers like Miroslav Satan and Curtis Brown and a two-way centre in Michael Peca. And Hasek wasn't the only character on the team. Rob Ray was a great guy. He'd chirp anybody, he'd fight anybody, it didn't matter. But he was a great teammate. I became really good friends with Jason Woolley, who was a younger guy on the team. Stu Barnes lived in my neighbourhood, on Buttercup Drive. It was too good for me to let it slide. I just *had* to call him Buttercup.

I felt pretty good when I first arrived in Buffalo. I was getting more playing time than I had all season with the Blackhawks. The Sabres had a shot at a playoff spot and would need a strong finish if we were going to slip in. I put up 17 points in 11 games, playing on a line with Satan and Brown. We went on a nice run heading down the stretch—7–2–1 in our last 10 games—and edged out the Carolina Hurricanes for the final spot in the Eastern Conference. I was contributing again, and it felt great—until I came down with a terrible stomach virus.

I missed the final couple games of the season. My stomach got so swollen I could hardly bend over, and I lost 10 pounds. I'd never experienced anything like that in my life. I managed to get back for our first-round series against the Philadelphia Flyers, but I was still recovering and wasn't much help. In the little ice time I had, I was pushed around like I weighed 10 pounds. We ended up losing in five games.

After we were eliminated, I took a good, long look at my career and considered my plans for the future. I was going to be 37 years old heading into the final year of my contract in Buffalo. Despite my age, I'd still put up 73 points between Chicago and Buffalo that season, which tied me with Mats Sundin for 17th overall in NHL scoring. I still had some game left in me. But I was heading for knee surgery in the off-season, and it wasn't clear how much more my body could take.

I did think seriously about retirement. Part of me considered going to culinary and restaurant management school. I was intrigued by the notion of owning and running my own place. I'd taken some culinary courses in the off-season, and I even collected menus from restaurants I liked when I was on the road. It was a real passion of mine at the time. I also looked forward to spending time with my boys, Tyson and Jake, who were about to be four and two years old. I even told the press that the coming season would be my last.

But leaving the game was much harder than I thought it would be. By the time the 2000–01 season started, I was waffling on what I wanted to do at the end of the year. When the season opened, I was playing some of the best hockey I had in quite a while.

"There's a real pride factor here for me," I told the press at the time. "I want to go out with a bang."

Instead, I went down with a bad groin, which I had first tweaked while training in the off-season. After the first couple of months on the ice, I felt a sharp pain in my groin during a game. Whenever I'd lift my leg up to go over the boards, I would feel this burning sensation ripping down both sides of my inner thigh. It was brutal. I had to go through the door because I couldn't hop the boards. Off the ice, I couldn't walk properly. I'd walk around like a friggin' cowboy. An MRI showed that I had an inflamed disc. It's called a burner.

As difficult as it was to admit, I knew my body was shutting down. It was frustrating. My back was sore all the time, and I was walking like John Wayne with that goddamn groin thing. And I was getting less and less ice time. In my eyes, the more I played, the better I was. We weren't talking about playing 28 minutes now, but I wanted to play at least 14 to 16 minutes a game. So when I was only getting about seven or eight minutes a game, it got to me. I knew what my body needed. The more you sit when you're in your late 30s, the worse you get. After you've played a tough game for many years, your body starts to show rust at that age. It was frustrating because I felt I could do more, and I wanted to do more—but I just couldn't.

It was also a tough situation because I had played against Lindy Ruff. We were only a few years apart in age, and now he was my coach. Lindy and I didn't agree on everything, and while I knew he had a job to do, I was getting older and didn't really want to admit that. I didn't like that I was on my way out—and taking orders from Lindy rubbed me the wrong way. It was all my fault. I was bitter because I wanted to play more, but I was in my late 30s and wasn't a star anymore. I knew that, but I thought I could still contribute.

My linemate Dave Andreychuk and I were roommates in my second season in Buffalo. It was great to be reunited with Andy. We'd just laugh and tell stories about the good old days.

We were both in the same position: 37 years old and not really knowing if we were going to play all that much. We'd also been teammates in New Jersey, but we didn't play together aside from the occasional power play. But despite the success we had together in Toronto, we never played together on a regular shift. We never had the opportunity to play together on the same line.

Lindy knew how to get under our skin. He'd come by our hotel room and do curfew checks on Andreychuk and me all the time. We'd hear the knock at our door and I'd open it up a crack.

"Yes? Can I help you?" I'd say.

"Let me in," Lindy would say.

He'd come in and look around and make sure Andreychuk was there too. We were two 37-year-old guys. Where the hell were we going to go? Andy would just shake his head.

While I wasn't happy on the ice, I had no animosity towards the Sabres organization. In fact, our owner, John Rigas, was great for a laugh. He would come into the dressing room to see us, but he had no clue who we were. Every time he came in, he'd look up at the name tag above our stall and pretend to recognize us as he shook our hands. Once, I switched spots with Brian Campbell, who was just a young guy at the time. Rigas shook my hand and called me Brian. So I *knew* he didn't know us from Adam.

In the end, I missed 11 games that season and put up 38 points. I still had some good hockey left in me and could still contribute—11 of those points had come in 13 games in February. We made it to the second round of the playoffs, where we lost to the Pittsburgh Penguins in seven games. It was the 11th Game 7 I had played in my career, but this time I was barely a factor.

I loved the team in Buffalo, but I knew that if I returned at all in 2001–02, it wasn't going to be with the Sabres. I was frustrated with how I was being used. I was uneasy about growing older and wanted to prove I could still play. It was a lot like I'd always felt: if you don't think I can play, then fuck you—I'll prove you wrong. But as you get closer to 40, it's not always clear whether you're trying to prove that to the doubters or to yourself.

When I got home from that last game, I looked exhausted and broken. Amy took one look at me and said, "You're done, aren't you?"

"Yeah," I sighed, resigned to it.

With the season over and my contract up, the media speculated on my future. As we cleaned out our lockers at HSBC Arena, reporters asked if I had made a final decision on retirement. I told the press that I wasn't coming back.

"It's been a great ride," I said. "I've got no regrets."

I talked about settling into life beyond the game. Amy and I had bought a new place in Toronto, and I wanted the boys to settle in there. Maddie, now a teenager, still lived nearby. I had already purchased season tickets to Leafs games at the Air Canada Centre. Everything pointed to my career being done.

The news that I was done spread like wildfire. I was sitting at home the next day, watching TSN, when the sports ticker across the bottom of the screen flashed news that Doug Gilmour had retired. It didn't feel right. Articles popped up that read more like obituaries than anything else. It felt like they were ready to bury my career and mark it with a headstone. I didn't like it at all. Was I *really* done? After 18 years, could I just call it quits like that? Sure, I'd played hard the entire time and it had taken its toll. But I had always figured they'd have to carry me off the ice—or at least that I'd have to crawl off, when my body was broken and battered beyond use.

So a day after seemingly announcing my end, I walked it back. I announced I would take the summer to decide my future and that I'd consider any offers from teams that came in. I was close to leaving, but I wasn't ready to close the door all the way just yet. My body might have been asking me to retire, but I knew my heart was still in the game.

Was I done?

Hell, no.

20

ONE MORE TRY

In September 2001—shortly after that terrible day on 9/11—I was still thinking hard about my life and my future. I went to an exhibition game at the Air Canada Centre—I wore a hat to try to avoid detection—and sat a few rows up from the glass as the game went on in front of me, without me.

I was 38 years old and had already played for six NHL teams. All the moving was taking a toll, and there was a real appeal to settling down. We were based out of Toronto at the time. My boys were five and three years old. Part of me wanted to just be a dad for a while. But another part of me wanted to prove that I still had what it took to compete.

I had been on the ice about once a week and worked out every day through the summer, but not in the way I usually had. I certainly wasn't in any condition to step back into a game.

But as I sat there, listening to the roar of the fans, watching the game flow up and down the ice, I knew I still wanted to be out there. I couldn't shake that feeling. By the second period, I had made up my mind. When I got home, I spoke with Amy about it, and she agreed that I still had some hockey left in me.

I called up Larry Kelly.

"You know what?" I said. "I think I'm going to start training a little bit harder."

"Okay," he said. "Let's think about this."

I told him to start putting out calls to see if any teams were interested in me. I was going to need a couple weeks to train on my own and get my legs back. I had to get my mind back into the game, too. I could feel my aging body creaking as I worked it back into shape. In the meantime, Kelly came back with two interested franchises: Ottawa and Montreal. Both were close enough to Toronto. It made sense to pursue both options.

As training camps wrapped up and the regular season got under way, I flew out to interview with the teams. Ottawa was interesting. They had a great team at the time: Zdeno Chara, Jason Spezza, Marian Hossa, Wade Redden. They were coming off a 109-point season, first in the Northeast Division and second in the Eastern Conference. Bottom line, they were a better team than the Canadiens at the time. In hindsight, the Senators would have offered a better chance of winning. Jacques Martin, my old coach from St. Louis, was behind the bench there, too, and I loved playing for Jacques. So there was a lot of interest in going there. But I was asking for $1.6 million for a one-year deal, and they weren't sure if they could come up with that kind of money. Times were tight for the Senators.

At the same time, Montreal was in Ottawa for a game. I went to meet general manager André Savard and coach Michel Therrien at Larry Kelly's office after the morning skate. They said they'd love to have me. Their star centre, Saku Koivu, had been diagnosed with cancer and was going to have to take some time away from the game to get better. There was a clear role for me to play there. They offered me $1.8 million. It took me about 12 hours to decide.

The day of my first practice in Montreal, I missed my exit and ended up being a half hour late. Brian Savage and Craig Rivet were both waiting for me in the lobby, ready to welcome me. So I was off to a great start!

The Habs had a good locker room. We had José Théodore and Jeff Hackett in net. And we had guys like Francis Bouillon, Patrice Brisebois, Gino Odjick, Richard Zednik, Stéphane Quintal and Craig Rivet. It was a fun team. We had French-Canadian players, Europeans, Americans and guys from English Canada. And it was good for me, too, because they didn't have high expectations. I was just another body that could maybe get some points here and there and help out on the power play.

After a road loss in Washington on a Saturday night, I made my debut in Montreal against my old team, the Buffalo Sabres. I played just over 20 minutes and was used heavily on the power play, and man, I could feel it. I was running on pure adrenaline, and I was completely exhausted at the end.

Afterwards, I got a real sign of where I was in my career. I'd set up Richard Zednik for our only goal in a 3–1 loss, but not one member of the press asked me a question, aside from one French reporter who came up to me and said, *"Parlez-vous français?"*

"No," I said. And he walked away.

That said, the Montreal media were skeptical about me at first, but by the end of the season I had no problem with them.

We were off till the following Friday, when we headed to Buffalo. I really wanted to beat my old team, especially in their barn. Before each game, you'd put money up on the bulletin board, and it would go to whoever scored the winning goal. I wanted an extra incentive, so I went big and put up $5,000. During the game, Vaclav Varada ran over our goalie, José Théodore, and knocked him right out. I couldn't let that stand. I was up at the blue line when the collision happened. I skated in and caught Varada as he was going the other way, and I took him out at the knees. We both got tossed from the game with match penalties. Maddie was dating a hockey player named Evan McGrath at the time. They were a little bit late in getting to the rink. By the time they arrived, I was already out of the game. They came down and watched the rest of the game with me, so at least I got to hang out with them.

I ended up getting two games without pay for the hit. I also had to apologize to Varada on a conference call. I did, but I added that he took our goalie out. He said he didn't mean to do it. "Yeah, you did," I said. "I played with you."

The $5,000 I put up on the board went into the kitty for a year-end team party. So it ended up being an expensive night for me. But the good news was that I could at least take a two-game breather. I could finally catch my breath and get my timing back in practice.

It was all worth it.

It was a fun season. We had a great management and ownership team. George Gillett owned the team, and he had a great sense of humour. He always had different businesspeople coming to the rink to show them around. During one game, about five minutes before the warm-up, he walked by the hallway with a group of friends. There were two or three of us out in the hallway, getting ready. When I saw him coming down the hall, I decided I was going to pull a prank on him. I used a Synergy stick at the time, which had a plug at the top of the hollow shaft. I never used the plugs; mine always just had tape over the end. I grabbed a water bottle, peeled back the top of my shaft and poured all the water into my stick. George walked up and introduced us to his friends.

"George, these sticks that you're buying us are terrible," I told him. "Feel how heavy they are."

He took it from me.

"Oh my God," he said. "It *is* heavy."

"Not only that," I said, "it's warped! Take a look at it in the light."

So George lifted it up towards the overhead lighting to have a look. The water came pouring out, drenching his suit. He was soaked—and he just started howling! He thought it was funny. Right before the game, with his entourage. Any other owner would have been *pissed*. But George was great.

I was moved up to the second line after Christmas, so I got to play a lot more than originally anticipated. It had taken me over a month and a half—and 23 games—to score my first goal for Montreal, which was incredibly frustrating. But I was working my way back into it. I was happy to get the ice time, but I could feel the wear on my body. I'd actually start warming up for games half an hour before anybody else, just to get my muscles and joints moving. I wouldn't even do up my skates in the locker room. I'd slip them on and then lean over, tucking the tongues underneath the shin pads—and then I'd wait until after the warm-up, when I was loose. I'd actually skate all through warm-up with my laces tucked in but not tied. Afterwards, I'd get to the bench and prop my foot up on the boards. I didn't want my teammates to notice what I was doing. Whenever I took my gear off, or tried to bend down to get my skates off—oh boy, did I ever feel like shit. After games, I'd cover myself in that heat rub—all over my back and legs. Or I'd just sit in the hot tub and soak.

I knew I wasn't what I once was, but my goal was to end the year with about 50 points. I played hard, trying to make my mind ignore my body. I was constantly talking my body into getting the job done. I was 180 pounds and 38 years old, but I wouldn't let anybody see that I was hurting. I was going to get in there and prove I belonged. In the end, I finished with 41 points in 70 games, which was decent for an old guy like me.

That April, I got into my first bar fight in quite a while. We were in Pittsburgh, where we'd just beaten the Penguins 3–0. With six games to go, we were holding on to the last playoff spot, with Washington, the Rangers and Buffalo close behind. After the game, eight of us met up at the bar at the William Penn Hotel to talk about what we needed to do down the stretch. A little guy wearing a Penguins sweater came over and wanted to talk to us. We told him, "Not right now." We just wanted to have a beer and hang out. The guy wasn't happy with us. Afterwards, I headed for the bathroom, and as I walked into the lobby, the little guy came up to me with a buddy who was tattooed up, probably about six foot two, around 220 pounds.

"Oh boy," I thought. They were hammered and looking for a fight.

I was wearing a suit; I was in no position to get into a fight. Nevertheless, the big guy threw a punch at me. I ducked under it and tackled him. I was on top of him, not letting him up, because he was huge. I couldn't afford to let him up! Meanwhile, the little guy was kicking me in the head. My teammates came running into the lobby, along with security guards. One of our guys sucker-punched the little guy. He got up with a busted nose and took off.

My suit was all ripped. It was a mess. I couldn't change because we weren't staying at the William Penn (team policy didn't allow us to drink in the bar of our own hotel). Security asked if we wanted to press charges if they caught the guys, but I said no. It wasn't worth it. We just went back to our chairs and had another beer, me with my ripped suit and bloodied face.

We managed to hold on to that last playoff spot and ended up playing Boston, the number one seed, in the first round. Koivu returned from his treatment for non-Hodgkin's lymphoma in time for the playoffs. Just a few months earlier, he'd been bald and thin from eight chemotherapy treatments. It was a remarkable, inspiring return, and it really fuelled our team. I think we took Boston by surprise.

After we split the first two games in Boston, the series shifted to the Molson Centre, where the home crowd went wild for Koivu. We trailed 3–1 going into the third period, and we looked beat. During the intermission, I told the guys we had to pull it together. We couldn't let the Bruins embarrass us in our own rink. It seemed to work. Donald Audette scored seven minutes into the third period to pull us within one. Then, under a minute later, I scored to tie the game. A few minutes later, Koivu scored the game winner on Byron Dafoe. The crowd erupted. We added an empty-netter to close out the game, winning 5–3.

We went on to win the series in six games, shocking the Bruins.

In the second round, we came up against the Carolina Hurricanes. I was playing on a line with Richard Zednik and Oleg Petrov. We had a good thing going. In Game 4 at home, Zednik got knocked out, which really set us back. We battled hard, but they had a three-games-to-two lead heading into Game 6 in Montreal. At 5:01 of the second period, I got called for tripping. I didn't agree with the call, and I was pissed off because we were down 5–1 at the time and it looked like our season was done. I shared a few words with the ref and then took my seat in the penalty box. I wasn't quite finished our conversation, so I slammed the door of the penalty box in frustration, just to make one last point. As soon as I slammed the door, the glass shattered. I'd never seen that happen before. I didn't know what to do. I thought, "Shit, I'm in here forever now." I put my head down in my hands and looked at my skates, as though I hadn't seen it happen. It ended up being one of the most viewed highlights of my career. But I swear, I couldn't make it happen again if I tried! I ended up getting an extra 10.

We lost the game, 8–2, and the series. The Hurricanes went on to beat Toronto in the Eastern Conference final and then lost to the Detroit Red Wings in the Stanley Cup Final.

After we were knocked out, George Gillett threw a party at his mansion. When everyone was gathered, he pushed in a wheelbarrow filled with the broken glass from the penalty box. He got me back!

"Here you go," he said. "You can take it home with you."

After the season, the general manager, André Savard, called me and said they wanted me to come back. My one-year deal had expired, but they thought they could get some use out of me for one more run. I agreed right away. I was thrilled to be coming back.

We had training camp in Colorado that September, near where the Gillett family had a mansion. I called up George's son Foster.

"Do me a favour," I said. "I can't stay in a hotel in training camp. It's not good for my body. I need to stay at your dad's house."

"Really?" he said.

"Yeah, I don't like the hotels," I said, making it seem like I was being a real diva about it. "I've always stayed in a house."

"Oh, okay," he said.

He bought it for a while. But then he figured out I was just joking around. At the end of training camp, the family invited the team to come up to their house and have a small party. We took three busloads of players, with all the rookies and staff and everyone. When we pulled up to the entrance, there was a carved wooden sign, about 10 feet by 10, that said, "Gilmour's House."

Everybody on the bus turned around and looked at me as if to say, "What the hell is this?"

"Don't even ask," I said.

I had to give Foster credit. I thought I had him, but he turned it right back around on me.

During the party, we asked George to show us his wine cellar. He happily obliged. About 10 of the veterans followed him down into a massive room filled with wine. It wasn't a cellar. It was like an entire basement.

"Come on, let's open up a couple of these," I said.

George happily obliged. He didn't open up just one bottle—he opened up eight right away. And these weren't just any bottles of wine. They probably averaged about $1,000 each. We were having a great time.

"Let's open another bottle," he said. He didn't give a second thought to it. We were probably drinking three glasses to a bottle. And he kept opening them up. We probably drank 50 grand down there. Honest to God, George was one of the best owners I ever played for.

The Canadiens struggled through the 2002–03 season. We had high hopes after Koivu's return and with José Théodore in net, after he won the Hart Trophy the season before. But we couldn't get things going. By early February, it was clear we weren't really in the playoff picture. But the thought that I might be traded didn't come up once. It wasn't even on my mind. The people in Montreal were great. The fans were wonderful. They were so passionate. Everyone understood that I didn't speak French, and no one gave me a hard time about it. The press didn't really want to talk to me much anyway, given that I was a 39-year-old fourth-liner. I wasn't a superstar anymore. I was seeing the game from a much different perspective. It was full circle, really. It was almost like I was a rookie again. I understood that I wasn't going to play that much. I mean, from my perspective, of course, I wanted to play more. But from their perspective, they probably got as much as they possibly could out of me.

A short time later, Pat Quinn, the Toronto Maple Leafs' coach and general manager, called Savard and inquired about whether they'd make a deal for me.

Savard called Larry Kelly to see if I'd be interested in possibly returning to Toronto. The Leafs were making another push for the playoffs and could use an extra body. And of course, there was my connection to the city. It was clear that I was going to be a third- or fourth-line player. Quinn wanted to know if I would accept the role. I said, "Absolutely—100 per cent." The deal wasn't done yet, but they knew I was open to it.

In truth, part of me was conflicted. I was 39 years old. It was clear that this could be my final season. As a player, you have a sense of just how good the team you're playing for is. The Habs were four or five points out of the playoffs at the time. Toronto was already pretty much a lock to make the playoffs again, and they had a pretty good lineup. But I knew what going there meant: this would be my last kick at it. I'd never fully admit it, but deep inside, I knew where things were heading. There was no avoiding it.

In the end, though, if this *was* going to be my last stretch, it was going to be pretty great to come back to the place that was really my home.

The day of the trade deadline, I called Larry and told him I was okay with the deal. I was supposed to get a bonus if we made the playoffs with the Habs, but the Leafs weren't going to be able to honour that. I agreed. Pulling on the Leafs sweater one more time would be worth it.

The Canadiens were on the road in Florida at the time. When I got off the ice after our morning skate, it was only 20 minutes before the deadline, so part of me thought that the trade wasn't going to happen after all. Things often fall apart like that. I checked my phone. There was a message from Larry. The deal was done. He told me that Pat Quinn was going to call me. I went into the locker room and told my teammates that I hadn't asked for the trade, but that I was on my way out. I told them how much I had appreciated those last two seasons with them. They were great teammates. Management was great. Ownership was great. I was proud to be a Hab.

My phone rang. It was Pat Quinn. The Big Irishman welcomed me home.

21
GOING HOME

It wasn't the homecoming I wanted. My first game back with the Toronto Maple Leafs also turned out to be my last.

I flew from Florida to Montreal and grabbed some suits. The next day, I was on a plane to Calgary, where the Leafs were on a western road trip. I didn't arrive in town until about two o'clock, and then I had a quick press conference. Later, I grabbed dinner with Gary Roberts and a bunch of the other guys from the team that I had known over the years. It was neat to be back in Calgary with Gary, after we'd been neighbours there when we played for the Flames all those years ago.

The next day, I pulled on a Leafs sweater. It felt weird to be playing my first game with Toronto in Calgary against the Flames. Things have a way of coming full circle.

I was exhausted from having just been on a road trip through California and then to Florida with the Canadiens. I really needed some time off before I played. I wasn't ready to go; my legs weren't there. But the Leafs had a bunch of injuries and they needed me in the lineup right away. Quinn put me on a line with Nik Antropov and Robert Reichel. I played the first period and felt pretty good, but I missed a good scoring opportunity. Then I stepped on the ice for my first shift of the second period, and I ran into Dave Lowry at the blue line. He caught me awkwardly and my knee just sort of snapped backwards.

I went down hard. I knew it was bad right away. I'd never had that kind of injury before. It felt like a charley horse; a really, really bad charley horse. I couldn't stand up, but I didn't want them to blow down the play. So I crawled towards the bench. I was going to get off the ice on my own. When I got to the bench, our trainer had me walk back and forth in the hallway. It felt like the pain was leaving. It felt like good news. Then our trainer told me to drag my toe. As soon as I did, I fell flat on my ass.

"I know it's sore," I said, "but it should be okay, right?"

He told me I was going to need an MRI. He said it was likely my medial collateral ligament (MCL) and possibly my anterior cruciate ligament (ACL).

"You're friggin' kidding me," I thought.

We flew to Vancouver that night, and then the next day I flew back to Toronto with Gary Roberts, who was also hurt. I wanted to avoid the media because we didn't know how bad it was. I was wearing a hoodie and track pants when I ran into them. I didn't have crutches, but I had a brace on and I was limping. I said, "Not now, guys."

I went straight to see my own doctor. It wasn't a team doctor. He took fluid out of my knee with a needle, to reduce the swelling. That way, when I went for the MRI, it would be easier to see what the damage was. The results came back: my ACL was torn and needed to be replaced, and my MCL was also damaged.

The surgeon took a piece out of my hamstring and used it as my new ACL. The operation was kind of a quick fix for older guys. I really just needed the knee to hold up for the time being. I wanted to fast-track the rehab, because the playoffs were right around the corner. If it had been the ACL alone, I could play while wearing a brace. But because the MCL was also affected, I wasn't able to push off to skate.

A recovery period of four to six weeks would take us right up to the playoffs, so I held on to the hope that I could make it back after all. I went for rehab sessions at the ACC two or three times a day, trying my best to get back into game shape. If the injury had happened around Christmastime, I'd have had a fighting chance at coming back in time for the playoffs, but at this point it was just going to take too long. I knew that, but I didn't want to admit it.

I started skating a bit, and the knee was feeling good. But just before the playoffs, the doctor took me aside and gave me the bad news. "It's not ready," he said. "You can't play."

It was a brutal feeling. I sat on the sidelines as the Leafs lost in the first round to the Philadelphia Flyers.

It was disappointing. I'd played only one period as a Maple Leaf before my knee had blown out. Now I wasn't sure if I was going to make it back onto the ice again. I started working out with Gary Roberts at his gym at Union Station right away. I didn't know whether Toronto was going to invite me back, and I gave some thought to whether I wanted to go somewhere else the following season or simply shut it down. I'd just finished my 20th year. I was coming off of major surgery. I was training and rehabbing, thinking that there might be a chance I could continue to play. But in my heart, I didn't know.

I was a long way away. I wasn't young anymore. An injury like that sticks with you. Could I put my body through that? That was my biggest concern. I didn't want to get back on the ice right away, because I wanted to get my knee even stronger. But people were asking. Gary was asking. Mom and Dad were asking. Amy was asking. My teammates were asking.

I just wasn't sure. I didn't want to say no and I didn't want to say yes. I had to think about it.

Then, that August, the press asked John Ferguson Jr., the Leafs' general manager, whether or not I'd be back for another year.

He said no, they didn't have any room for me.

That's when I knew it was over. The decision was made for me. There was no way I was going to move again and play in another city. And with my recovery from knee surgery, it was unlikely a team would have serious interest anyway.

I dialed Larry Kelly's number. We had a long chat. It was a hard decision.

"Look, there's no room for me in Toronto," I said. "It's time."

"Gilly," Kelly said, "if you've had enough, it's a pretty good career."

We made arrangements to announce my retirement. It was refreshing when I made that decision. I had complete control. We put a press release out and announced what day we were going to make the announcement. I called my parents. They were already in the loop on what I was thinking because I'd spent the summer out at the lake, travelling back and forth from Kingston to Toronto in between rehab sessions. Dad was always asking me what I was going to do. He wanted me to play again. And there was a part of me that wanted to do it for him, to work as hard as I could, step back on the ice in the NHL for one last season and go out the right way. I'd wanted him to see me play one last time. But now I had to tell him he wouldn't be able to.

We made arrangements for my big farewell. I had only played one period with the Leafs, so I felt I hadn't really been a part of the team, and I decided not to have a press conference down at the rink. This was just about me, now. We held it at the Rosewater, a restaurant in downtown Toronto. I invited some of my close friends and guys I had played with. Tie Domi was there, and he said a couple of words. Grant, my accountant, was there. Gary Roberts was there. Amy was there.

Larry Kelly had told me, "If you cry, I'm going to punch you." So my number one goal was not to be upset and not to cry. I came close, but I held it in. I had to be positive about it. After all, I did play 20 seasons. I was fortunate to get that many.

I thanked every person I could remember. I made it official. And when it was done, it felt like a piano had been lifted off my back. I felt no regrets. When I was done with the press conference, I had all my close friends meet me over at Harbour Sixty, a steakhouse not far from the Air Canada Centre, in the basement. I bought them all steaks and drinks. I did an interview for Bob McCown's radio show while we were there. I'd had a few glasses of wine by then, so I was nice and relaxed—not nervous at all—and I was on the air for about 20 minutes. (Bob and I had known each other for years. We'd been co-owners of a restaurant in the early '90s, and we once did a commercial for his radio show together. A few years after I retired, Bob even bought my house.)

It was good. It was right. It was the end.

22

GAME OVER

It's a strange feeling to be 40 years old and finished with the career you spent your entire life preparing for.

You find yourself asking, "Okay, so now what am I going to do with the rest of my life?"

One of the first things I did was quit my gym membership at Station 7. If I was retired, I wasn't working out with Gary Roberts anymore!

About three months later, I played in a men's hockey league in north Toronto, a Thursday night game at eight o'clock. Some of the guys I knew from a local bar near my house in Leaside asked me to join their team. These were guys I would sit with for hours at Originals Ale House, having beers and just hanging out. I couldn't turn them down. It was a pretty fun league. Former Leaf Nick Kypreos, who lived in the area, played in it, too.

I suited up for one game—and got tossed out for fighting.

The guys in the league were probably five to 10 years older than I was. I wasn't trying to be competitive. I didn't take any shots. I just tried to set up plays and have fun. I didn't want to show anybody up or embarrass anyone. It's all about going for beer afterwards, anyway. Hanging out.

But one of the guys kept slashing me every time I went to the net, and it was pissing me off. Eventually, I had had enough, so I turned around and punched him. He went down with a bit of embellishment. The ref blew his whistle and said, "You can't do that! You're gone!"

"Of course, I am," I thought. "I'll never play another game in this league again, thank you."

For the second time that year, I was retired!

I spent a couple of years away from the game. I tried to get involved in a couple of business ventures. First, I built a house in Toronto's Forest Hill neighbourhood, which I later sold to Mats Sundin. After that, I got connected with a mortgage company called Monster Mortgage and spent some time being part of the management side of the company while focusing on representing it.

Then, in 2006, John Ferguson Jr. called me to his office at the Air Canada Centre and asked me if I wanted to join the franchise in an advisory role. It was an incredible opportunity My heart was still in the game; I missed it and wanted to find a way back in. I started to sit in on meetings with management, learning about the game from a whole new perspective. I was part of the activity on trade deadline day, stuff like that. I realized that the front office does so much more work than we usually give them credit for. We had to keep track of all the players in the organization's system, understanding who was where and what the plan was for them. It was a lot of fun.

When Ferguson was relieved of his duties in 2008, Cliff Fletcher stepped in. He put me into a role where I would go and watch players the Leafs had drafted and give my opinions on them. It got me back into a rink, and I really enjoyed it. I went to places like Russia and Sweden, and I'd watch our farm team, the Toronto Marlies, all the time, just getting a handle on what the team was up to. I'd shadow Cliff and get a sense of what his role was—how he talked to other GMs and how he managed the organization. It wasn't like I had a lot of clout. It was more of a learning experience for me than anything.

After that, the Leafs gave me the title of director of player development. I did more travelling. I went and saw Leafs prospect Nikolay Kulemin in Moscow with scout Mike Penny.

Again, it was a great opportunity. But after a while, the travel became a bit much. I wanted to spend more time at home and get more involved with the team directly. In 2008, an assistant coaching vacancy opened up with the Marlies. Greg Gilbert was the head coach. Cliff asked me if I wanted to take a shot at it. I had always wondered what it might be like to coach. There had been so many coaches that I admired over the years, and I wanted to see the game from that angle. I felt like I'd have something positive to offer.

It was a unique opportunity. I had never played a single game in the minors—I went straight from junior to the NHL back in 1983. I didn't know what it was like to play there. Now, I was hopping on a bus with the Marlies, travelling all over the place. My job was to look at the other teams' penalty-killing tendencies and come up with a plan for our power-play unit. Joe Patterson, the other assistant coach, focused on penalty killing.

There were some guys on the team and in the league that I had played with. But since I had crossed over into management, it meant I couldn't hang out with them in bars the way I once would have. I had to be serious! Again, I was just trying to learn, to soak it all in.

Maddie's boyfriend, Evan McGrath, had been drafted by Detroit in 2004 and was playing for their farm team in the American Hockey League, the Grand Rapids Griffins, at the time. He and Maddie were living there together. The Griffins came to town to play a couple weeks into the season, and they kicked our asses. It was rough; being beaten by your future son-in-law's hockey team. Evan kept looking over at me from the visitors' bench, but I wouldn't look at him. I was sour. Apparently, I'd forgotten to retire my competitive streak.

That November, at about 8 a.m., I was driving to the Marlies' rink in Etobicoke for a practice when I got a call. It was the coach and general manager of the Kingston Frontenacs, Larry Mavety. Larry had given me my start in Junior A hockey with the Belleville Bulls, and he was still a close friend after all these years. He asked me if I wanted to come out to Kingston and take over from him as the team's head coach, while he focused on the general manager's role. We'd had brief discussions about it before, but this time it was serious. He wanted to know that day—he wanted to step aside and put me on the bench right away.

It was a tough decision. My relationship with Amy had slowly dissolved over time, and we had divorced in 2005. Despite that, we were still a tight-knit family, and our boys, Tyson and Jake, were going to school in Toronto. A little while after the divorce, I met someone new. Sonya Victoria took my breath away, right away. She was funny, kind and drop-dead gorgeous. Sonya had a career as a professional singer and hair stylist. We met in Hamilton and hit it off immediately. I fell hard and fast for her. It wasn't long before we were engaged and had a beautiful daughter, Victoria, who is just as vibrant and lovely as her mom. I was thrilled to be a dad yet again. Now I had two wonderful daughters and two incredible sons. And I was in the midst of pursuing a new career, coaching at one of the highest levels in the game. It seemed that everything was settled in my life. But this opportunity pulled at me. I liked the thought of returning to Kingston, to coach in the city where I grew up, a city that still held such a strong place in my heart after all these years.

And, of course, there were my parents. They were living in a condo in downtown Kingston, right by the water. My older sister Debbie and brother David were both still living in town. (Donna and her husband lived in Oshawa.) Mom and Dad went to Frontenacs games all the time at the new K-Rock Centre downtown. I thought about all the time we'd shared in rinks together over the years. I thought about those early days, when Mom helped me skate and Dad put me on defence. I even thought about the mashed potatoes and Ensure—this time, the thought made me smile.

I'd spent so much time in my life being on the road, being a professional hockey player, living my own life. I wanted to slow it down. We'd had great times over the summers in Loughborough Lake, where my parents still came to visit after selling their own place and moving into the condo. I wanted more of that, and I didn't know how much time I'd have left with them.

So instead of going to the rink that morning, I called up Greg Gilbert and told him I had to go see Cliff Fletcher down at the Air Canada Centre. We sat down in his office and chatted for about half an hour. I told Cliff that I was thinking about taking the position, and the reasons why, and he was fully supportive. After leaving Cliff's office, I called Sonya and told her what I was thinking. She was behind me, too. As I drove back to the Marlies' practice in Etobicoke, I continued to turn the idea over and over in my mind, and by the time I had arrived at the rink, my mind was made up.

It was just after 10 a.m., and practice was still going on. I went over to the bench and called over to Gilbert. I told him what was happening, and then said my thank-yous and goodbyes. I'd only been there for two months, so it was kind of weird. Then I called up Larry Mavety and told him I would accept the job. They wanted me in Kingston by 2 p.m. because they were calling a press conference. With not much time to spare, I rushed back to my place, grabbed a couple of suits and packed a bag, and hit Highway 401, eastbound for Kingston.

While I was driving, I called up my dad.

"What's going on?" Dad asked.

"I'm coming home," I said.

"Oh, that's good," he said. He had no clue what I was talking about.

"I'm coming to Kingston to work," I said.

"Okay, what are you talking about?" he laughed. "You're coaching the Marlies. Why would you come to Kingston?"

"I'm going to coach the Frontenacs," I said.

There was a pause. Dad wasn't a man of many words. All he said was, "Oh, okay." But I knew how excited he was. There are many ways to look at my decision, in hindsight. I probably would have had a more direct path to coaching or management at the highest levels of the game if I had stayed with the Marlies. But I'd never see it that way. I was going home—and that's all that really mattered.

23

BIG LEAGUE

For the next four years, Dad criticized my hockey sense. And I loved every minute of it.

It was just like when I was playing. He'd voice his opinion to me about coaching. I'd dig in and give him a hard time in return about it, but I actually enjoyed the banter. It was kind of our thing.

"You put the wrong guy on the power play," he'd say. "You used the wrong system on that penalty kill."

"Thanks, Don," I'd reply.

Mom and Dad lived five minutes away from the rink. If it was nice out, they would walk home together. If it was snowy, I'd give them a ride home. But either way, they were always there. If I had a day off, we'd go out for lunch somewhere. It was nice. Remember, I left home when I was 17 years old.

I still had the cottage I'd bought in 1997, so we'd had the chance to spend time together in the summertime, but this was different. It was pretty much every day. It's one aspect of my decision that I'll never regret.

I had my own coaching philosophy going in, but it quickly evolved. A coach has to absorb everything. I have to listen to my assistants, I have to listen to my general manager, and I have to listen to my players. Coaches aren't always right! You have to do it your way, but you have to consider input from everybody. I had to learn about mixing lines and adjusting game plans on the fly. I had to rethink the game in many ways.

I was a player's coach. At least I *wanted* to be. I didn't want to be a hard-ass. I wanted to get the best out of my players, game in and game out. My approach to doing that was to pat them on the back. You made a mistake—try not to make it again. That kind of thing. I wanted them to know that the number on the back doesn't matter; it's what's on the front of the jersey. I wanted to inspire them.

"Your junior career is going to go by quick," I told them. "So do your best and work hard each and every day."

I only held half-hour practices, but they were hard. There was no dogging it. I wanted them to practise the way we played.

But soon I learned that I was going to have to be a hard-ass at times. I quickly discovered that the nice-guy approach doesn't always cut it. Sometimes you can't just pat them on the back; you have to shout in their ear and let them know that if they do that again, they'll be sitting on their ass for the rest of the game. That was a throwback lesson from Pat Burns. But at the same time, I always thought it was important to remember that at the end of the day, these players were still just kids. They're 16 to 20 years old. We had to have rules and structure. So, we were enforcing a curfew every night and making sure we stayed on top of them with their schooling. I had to understand the pressure that they are under at that age, even while playing hockey at a high level.

The only thing that was really hard about coaching the Frontenacs was that I didn't get to see my kids as much as I had hoped. It was hard not being there in Toronto. Sonya and Victoria stayed with me in Kingston on the weekends, returning to Toronto during the week. The hardest part about the move was the time that I was spending away from my boys again. Jake and Tyson were both playing minor hockey. I tried to get down to see them every Sunday night and Monday. Then it was back on the road to Kingston at 6 a.m. on Tuesday morning. It was a lot of driving.

After my third year coaching in Kingston, I had a meeting with the Frontenacs' owner, Doug Springer. He wanted me to take over as general manager of the franchise, because Larry Mavety was moving into retirement. I didn't think I could do both jobs. But the idea of moving into a managerial role held a lot of appeal for me. It meant I could be on the road to see my family more. It was also a new challenge. To take over the head-coaching position, I brought in my old teammate and friend Todd Gill.

Being general manager was a whole new experience. I was able to take a big-picture view of the club. I leaned on my experience working in the Leafs' front office to help guide me. But managing a major junior hockey club is a lot different from the NHL. There are so many factors you have to consider when it comes to recruiting and drafting players, trading guys who are still in high school, managing your staff and budget, all while trying to make sure the product on the ice is great for the fans. I was fortunate to have the help of a great support staff, especially Darren Keily, our director of hockey operations, who joined the team in 2011.

On top of all that, there were fans and parents asking about every decision I made. It was way different than when I played. The Ontario Hockey League has evolved into a league run by agents and parents. There are some parents who will step in and prevent their kid from playing for an organization they don't like, or who have already made under-the-table agreements with other teams to try to prevent you from drafting their kid. There's a lot of politics involved in junior hockey today that didn't seem to be there when I was playing. Or maybe it was a factor, and I just wasn't aware of it. But it certainly is a complicated business.

While I was coaching in Kingston, I learned that Pat Burns was battling incurable cancer. The last time I saw Pat was about a month before he died. Dave Ellett and I flew in to visit him just outside of Montreal, near a rink that was being built and named in his honour. Pat had already fought cancer so valiantly, with the same spirit he showed as a coach. He survived a scare with colon cancer in 2004 and then liver cancer in 2005. But four years later, the damn disease had returned and had metastasized in his lungs. There was nothing else to do.

He was maybe 125 pounds and could barely walk, but he was happy to see us. We shared stories about the 1993 team. We had some good laughs together. We talked about all the characters and all the shit we used to get into. He talked about how much fun that team was. Our playoff run was still fresh in his mind. We were so close.

Pat had gone on to win the Stanley Cup with the New Jersey Devils in 2003. We talked about how great it was that he was able to win it in the end, because that's what we all aspired to do.

When he coached in Toronto, Pat would always go back to Quebec in the summertime, to a cottage he owned in a secluded wooded area. He loved his privacy. He loved sitting by the waterfront. He was surprising that way. He would go out in public once in a while, but he generally hid from the spotlight. He wanted his downtime—and I get that now, because I'm like that, too.

We had kept in touch over the years after our time together in Toronto. Every time I played against his team, he would try to get under my skin, yelling at me from the bench or complaining to the ref about me. He'd give one of his guys the job of pestering me on every shift, shoving me after the whistle and stuff like that. "Go tell Burnsie to fuck off," I'd tell whichever guy he had on me that game.

Pat had earned so much respect around the league. The man had paid his dues, working his way up from being a part-time scout with the Hull Olympiques in the Quebec Major Junior Hockey League. He later became an assistant coach and then head coach of the Olympiques, before moving up to become the coach of the Sherbrooke Canadiens, the Habs' farm team in the AHL. He moved up to the top job with the Canadiens the following year, in 1988–89—winning the Jack Adams Award but losing in the Stanley Cup Final to our Flames team—and the rest is history.

But that day, he wasn't the gentle giant we remembered. He was fading. He said he was tired and that he just couldn't do chemo again.

"I just can't do it anymore," he said.

Pat died on November 19, 2010. It was gutting to see that gentle giant go. But he fought so hard, and he finally deserved some rest.

I thought of him when I got the call several months later to say that I had been inducted into the Hockey Hall of Fame. Pat should have been inducted already—and everyone knew it. He'd be elected posthumously a few years later, but it's a shame he didn't get to experience the honour while he was alive.

...

The news that I was heading into the Hall caught me off guard. It was such an incredible honour. I didn't know what to say. I went in with my old teammate Joe Nieuwendyk, as well as Ed Belfour and Mark Howe. The weekend of the induction ceremony, I was incredibly nervous. My family came out to be part of the event. Beforehand, I was pacing back and forth at the hotel because I was so nervous about my speech.

At the event, they always have someone special introduce you and read out your bio. You don't know who it will be until that moment. I have to admit that I was surprised when Tie Domi came out. He's always been a friend, but he wasn't someone who had a significant impact on my career. He and I had also had it out because I drafted his son Max eighth overall for the Frontenacs that year, but Tie had wanted him to go to the London Knights. He called me up, all pissed off that I had drafted Max. But I had picked the best player available and done what was right for my franchise. I ended up trading Max to the Knights for three second-round draft picks. But it was a frustrating experience for us both. Anyway, I like Tie, but there were a lot of other people who could have introduced me into the Hall of Fame.

I was still trying to process that when I started my speech.

"Can anyone tell me who that was speaking?" I began. "I haven't seen him in a couple of years. Last I spoke to him, I drafted his son . . ."

The crowd let out a muffled laugh.

But then I looked at my family in the crowd and tried to settle in. I'd played 20 seasons. I'd scored 450 goals and had 964 assists. All things considered, 1,414 career NHL points wasn't bad for a guy who went 134th overall. It was a special moment for me and my family. After all those years of trying to prove everyone wrong, especially as a kid and through junior, it was surreal to be standing there at that podium in Toronto, having been included among the best players ever to take to the ice. It was humbling. I wanted to acknowledge that there were so many people along the way who had helped me get to that point. I certainly couldn't mention them all—obviously, I had played with a lot of teams along the way—but I tried my best.

I spoke about playing minor hockey, when my dreams were just to make it to junior. From there, the NHL was in sight. Once I got there, I learned how many people have to hold you up to have a successful career. I spoke about Larry Mavety, who had given me that first opportunity with the Belleville Bulls all those years ago. He believed in me. And Gord Wood, who drafted me for the Cornwall Royals, taking a chance on me when no one else would. I thanked Larry Kelly, who had been my agent for 22 years, and who had had my back through all of the ups and downs along the way. And Grant Skinner, my accountant, who helped me understand how to protect what I had earned and make sure I knew how to manage it properly.

Of course, I thanked my friend, Don Cherry—still biased, after all those years. And Cliff Fletcher, who taught me so much along the way, reaching all the way back to my time in Calgary. There were the coaches, the managers, the teammates, the training staff who pieced us back together. And there were all the fans—the heart that they showed us, and the intensity that they gave us. I thanked all the people who put up with my practical jokes through the years. I took some time to think about the friends we had lost along the way—guys like Peter Zezel and Bob Probert, as well as Sonya's father, Fernando Victoria. And then I thanked Pat Burns.

"We all miss him. The league misses him," I said. "More importantly, we believe he'll be here one day."

I was emotional when I moved on to my family. They were all there. Sonya, the love of my life. And my kids: Maddison, Jake, Tyson and little Victoria—the joys of my life. And there were my siblings, whom I was still so close to: Dave, Debbie and Donna. There were so many people in my family who mattered deeply to me. And finally, I looked at my parents, who both sat there with their hands perched on canes. My dad raised a hand to acknowledge me. "You believed in me," I said, and I started to tear up. "Thank you for letting me live my dream."

After the induction was over, I was exhausted. We skipped the post-ceremony parties and took the limo back to my house to sit back and enjoy the moment together. As we all sat around together, Debbie asked me if I had let it sink in yet.

"Do you realize what you've done?" she asked me. "Do you see it now?"

I looked at her and took a deep breath. Here I was, a few decades after I'd skated around the ice in my oversized gear, when they called me "Little Gilly." The journey from there had been so tough and so long. But I had made it. Now, I was in the Hall of Fame. It finally set in, and it felt great.

"Yeah," I said, with a sigh. "Now I know."

The following September, I sat in a hospital room in Kingston and watched my father die. He had been getting sick for some time; his diabetes had worn him down and the complications were finally taking their toll. He was 82 years old. When he was first admitted to the hospital, he came down with some infections, and we just knew that he wasn't getting out.

I came to visit right before the Frontenacs' home opener. He pulled me in close and called me "Douglas," like he always had. Then he gave me a thumbs-up, which meant "go get a win." He was coaching right to the end. We turned the game on in the room so he could watch.

He only lived for a few more days.

When Dad started to go, our whole family was there beside him. Any life support had been shut down, and we just wanted to stay with him until it was time to go. He wasn't in a rush. A nurse came into our room at Kingston General to check on him.

"Your dad, was he an athlete?" she asked.

We all smiled sadly. Don Gilmour? He was a Kingston legend.

"Yes," my mom said. "He was."

"Well," the nurse said, "his heart is very strong."

We were beside him for almost six hours, making sure he was never alone. Near the end, I pulled in close beside him and told him I loved him and gave him a kiss. I left the room when he died. I didn't want my family to see me cry.

I went to the funeral home on the west side of the city. I wanted to take care of everything—the funeral, the burial plot. In a way, that's how I coped with losing him. I just needed to take charge of things. I called the newspaper and made sure they had the details.

The visitation was jammed with people who knew and loved my dad. He was Kingston famous. We were there for hours.

At the funeral, we played his favourite song: "Big League" by Tom Cochrane. He always played it. We decided that I would give a eulogy. I spoke about all the good times: about mashed potatoes and Ensure, about having him as my coach, about the time Donna fell through the ice. I joked about how he'd stop by the strip club to visit his old inmate friends while Mom went shopping in Toronto. I spoke about all the advice he'd given me throughout my career: the near-daily phone calls, telling me what I needed to work on and what I should have done in the game I just played. He had bought satellite dishes through the years to make sure he could watch me play. He taped every game. He had at least five bins of games and commercials I had been in, which he kept stored up at my place on the lake. I talked about the cars he collected and sold.

There was no one quite like Don Gilmour; there was no one like my dad.

He was cremated, and we bought a plot in a memorial wall at a gravesite just off Sydenham Road, the route we always took on the way out of Kingston towards the lake. I wanted to be able to give him a wave every time I'd drive by.

A few days later, I was back at my place on Loughborough Lake, going through some of the old things Dad had kept in the garage. I flicked on a dusty old radio that I never used, to have some tunes to keep me company. Dad was a hoarder, and he stored all his stuff up at my place, so there was a lot to go through. He must have had a hundred $2 bills hidden away. And he had four or five thousand dollars stashed in his shaving kit. I also had five of his suitcases. One of them was full of what looked like old newspapers. They were all yellowed and aged. I started to shuffle through the pages. They were newspaper clippings from my entire career, going all the way back to my first years playing junior and pro.

All those old pages, collected by him, told the story of my life.

As I sat there poring over them, a familiar tune started playing on the radio. It was Dad's favourite song.

> When he was a kid, he'd be up at five.
> Take shots 'till eight, and make the thing drive.
> Out after school and back on ice.
> That was his life . . .
> He was going to play in the Big Leagues.
> Oh, oh . . . The Big Leagues.

I put down the yellowed newsprint, closed my eyes and started to cry.

"We made it, Dad," I thought. "We did. Thank you."

ACKNOWLEDGEMENTS

Thank you, Mom and Dad, for believing in me from the beginning and giving me everything I could possibly need in life. And to my siblings, Dave, Debbie and Barry, Donna and Neil, for being a constant support in my life.

To my children, with all my love. This is for Maddison, Evan and Elle. And for Jake, Tyson and Victoria. I'm so proud of you all.

Thank you, Sonya, for being my partner and my love. And thank you, Fernando, Belmira, Samantha, Carlos, Arlindo, Teresa and Johnny.

From the very beginning of my hockey career, I was lifted up by the friendship, support and guidance of so many. Thank you to all of my teammates along the way. To all the coaches who put up with me. To all the trainers and doctors who kept me going. And to the owners and managers who made it all possible. Thank you to my billets in Cornwall. To Gord Woods, Ron Caron, Odie, Bob and Deloris, Becky, Bart and Linda, and Chris. Thank you, Larry Kelly, for your wisdom and guidance through the years. And thank you, Cliff Fletcher, for believing in me.

Thank you, Robyne. And thank you to Amy Cable and the whole family. Thanks to my marketing manager and business partner, Kelly Gianopoulos, and her daughter Ella. And thank you to the team at Boon-Town.com. Thank you to my friends the Carlins, the Hadalls, the Odettes, the Holidays, Rino, the Anthonys, the Mercanti family, Jerry Montour and Kenny Hill, Dean Collett-Koi, Steve Davies, Bob Lieter, Bob Lavell, Grant Skinner and company, the Selbys, Eddie Menton, Shakey, Ron and Sandy, Scott Sutherland, Tammy and Ricky, the Di Donatos, the Fallettas and Wayne Cowley. To my late buddy Donnie Kruse and all the staff at Stanley's. To Scott Douglas at BMW Kingston. To Mav and Brenda, Mike Clairfield and Dr. Dave Greenburg.

Thank you, Dan Robson, Rick Broadhead, Jim Gifford and the rest of the team at HarperCollins Canada.

Thank you, Scott Sutherland, and Chris and Chris from Whitewater Brewing Company. Thank you, Grapes, for the biased Kingston love throughout my career. Thank you to Kerch, the scouts and all the Frontenacs staff. Thank you, Darren and Robin, MB and Kenny, Zack, George, Joe Five-O, Fink, Big T, Artie, Rene, the Springer family, Frank and Dom, Bridal Bash, Tom Cochrane, Jim Cuddy and Blue Rodeo, the Hip, the Barenaked Ladies, Tony, Colin, Peter, Dom, Terry, Rocky Richard and Os Crew. Thank you, Lucky, Andrew Jackson, Brian Green, Scotty McKay, John Kutz, Nick and Suzie. Thank you, the NHL Alumni Association, the staff at Kingston General Hospital and Trillium retirement home. Thank you, Conquistador, the Design to Perfection crew, the Coop, the Source and Wendy Alana Photography.

And thank you, the fans, for the love and support through the years. Thank you for taking the time to read this book. I hope you enjoyed it.

—DG

When I was about 10 years old, I went to my first Leafs game at Maple Leaf Gardens. Somehow my father had managed to get seats right behind Félix Potvin through the company he worked for. It felt like we'd won the hockey lottery. I don't recall what happened in the game, but I remember the players: the Cat, Clark, Killer and company. After seeing them on television, in trading cards and on posters on my wall, I was awestruck to see them live, skating in front of me. They were like superheroes. I remember trying to hang on to each moment in that stuffy old barn, watching the clock tick down, wishing I could freeze time. But it ended, as it always does, despite us. We pushed out onto Carlton Street, picked up some street meat, climbed into our Ford Explorer and drove away from that magical place, back to the suburbs. But my mind stayed there, in the Gardens, dreaming of one day playing on that hallowed ice as an NHL star.

In retrospect, those dreams seem completely ridiculous. But I thought about those memories as Doug and I wrote this book together. I sat next to him at Originals Ale House in Leaside, week after week, listening to the stories of his life. When we spoke about his family and youth in Kingston, I could see that, really, he'd been just like me—just like so many of us. Doug was a dreamer whose dreams came true. And, I came to realize, so was I—in a much different way, of course, but dreams are malleable; they may bend with time, but the substance remains the same.

So, this is for the people who make that possible—from the stars who set the course to the coaches, teachers and mentors who guide the journey. This is for the family and friends who fuel it. For those who put it all in perspective and help us alter the path towards whatever dreams come next.

Thank you, Doug, for giving me the opportunity to help share your story. Thank you, Rick Broadhead, for your constant support and guidance as a friend and agent. Thank you, Lloyd Davis, for your meticulous edits, and Patricia MacDonald, for your careful proofread. Thank you, Jim Gifford, and the wonderful team at HarperCollins Canada for your patience and confidence in this project.

Thank you, Jayme, for loving me despite me—and for holding this ship together, as always, with your constant sacrifice, guidance and brilliance. You are everything to me.

Thank you, Mom, Jai and Jenna, for your love and support. And thank you, Dad. I've stopped the clock in my mind. We're still sitting at the Gardens; you're still beside me. And I'm still dreaming because of you.

—DR